I0099384

The Guide

Ski Resorts

An expert's insights on ski resorts, ski towns,
skiing, and riding in the Rockies

Second Edition

Jordan Gale

All rights reserved. No portion of this book may be reproduced, stored in a retrieval system, or transmitted in any form or by any means – electronic, mechanical, photocopy, recording, scanning, or other – except for brief quotations in critical reviews or articles, without prior written permission of the author.

Copyright © 2017 Jordan Gale
All rights reserved.
ISBN:
ISBN-13: 9780692717226
ISBN-10: 0692717226

CONTENTS

Introduction

This book can help you identify the best mountains for you to ski and snowboard on. There are different types of mountains for different types of skiers and riders, and different personality types, so among other things, I hope that this book helps you figure out which mountains are best for you. If you don't have time to visit every ski resort, then the descriptions can help you find the resorts that are best suited for you.

This is also a book to illuminate the wonders of skiing and snowboarding. I hope that as you are reading this book, my words will help you to taste the sweetness of the skiing experience and will provide you with insights on how to make your future experiences better than they have ever been.

I hope that as your motivation to plan your next ski vacation increases, you not pick just any mountain that happens to be on your mind right now, but that you will go to the mountain that is best for you and whomever you are bringing with you.

Why

Skiing has made my life better. It's not only the exercise. It's not only the relationship building. It's not only the stress release. It's not only the happiness that overtakes me while I am skiing. It's more than the sunshine. It's more than the conversations that bring laughter or wisdom or growth. It's more than skill progression. It's more than immersion in nature. My skiing experiences have changed me for the better.

You may not have given it much thought, but you too are changed by how you spend your vacation time. You can be better off for having spent time at the right ski resort for you. I want to help you identify the resorts that will be the most beneficial to you.

As you read this book, you will discover how to best use your vacation time and where to spend your precious ski days.

The first half of this book is about ski resorts in the Rocky Mountain range. Each chapter covers every ski resort in a specific state, with the exception of Colorado, which has multiple chapters.

Every ski resort is perfect for a certain type of person. Therefore, I will do my best to describe not only the mountain and the resort, but also other aspects of the ski town that can help you to have the best vacation imaginable.

The second half of the book is commentary about topics that I am often asked about since I spend so much time at ski resorts. It covers everything from commentary on ski town culture, to tips on becoming a better skier, to information on gear.

Whether you prefer skis or a snowboard, this book is for you.

A note on the Second Edition

The second edition, finalized in 2017, is the most comprehensive book of its type. The ski resort industry is now changing constantly. When the first edition of this book was released, the largest ski resort in the United States, measured in inbounds acres, was Big Sky. Previous to Big Sky it was Vail Resorts. That changed for the 3rd time in less than 10 years when Park City and Canyons combined. Now if you want to go to the biggest inbounds resort, then Park City is your resort.

With this edition, I've updated statistics to help compare and contrast resorts. I've also gone back to resorts I hadn't been at in too long and added the latest information about those areas. For those of us that don't have as much vacation time as we would like, choosing the ideal ski resort for your next vacation could mean the difference between a good vacation and the best vacation ever.

1. Purpose

Skiing gives the cold weather a purpose. The cold is no longer a discomfort, but a welcome change that brings fun to the winter.

The wonders of the mountains go unnoticed by so many people. The cold, the hauling of equipment, the lift lines… to the casual observer, skiing might not seem as if it is that fun. Why would anyone pay a lot of money to hassle with equipment, and lug it to the slopes, only to stand in line in the cold? Therefore, the fact that millions of people ski is evidence that there is a payoff that is not easily observed from the condo window.

Here are comments given by skiers and riders that explain why the enjoyment far outweighs the challenges.

- ✓ "The camaraderie."
- ✓ "I get a great workout and I hardly notice that I am exercising."
- ✓ "There are pleasures in skiing: the physical pleasure of the float, or the flight, and the emotional pleasure of exertion, and being in nature."
- ✓ "I focus on skiing when I ski, so all the other problems and challenges in life disappear. Skiing is a respite, a haven."
- ✓ "It's fun. Why is it fun? I don't know. I don't question things that put a smile on my face."

The way that I feel about snow skiing is that it is the only thing that interrupts a normal life for the adventure, beauty and physical sensations that only snow skiing can provide. It is the source of a kind of pleasure that not everyone has experienced. Snow skiing is one of my favorite things in life. It can be that good for you too. I also enjoy snowboarding. Some days, snowboarding brings exactly the right feeling.

2. Learning in New Mexico

Even if you never had a burning desire to travel to New Mexico, making an effort to get to Taos Ski Valley is definitely worth the journey. I was very impressed with the ski school there. I have taken countless lessons throughout my life, so I don't always expect to learn something new when I take a lesson; I'm just trying to focus on good skiing habits to help me ski efficiently. I also like to have the ski instructor let me know whether I have started to develop any bad habits. To this day, I sometimes think about having the front of my boots "be headlights" that guide the direction of my turns, and I think about the smoothness of my turns - - that was my favorite tip at Taos.

Every day that I took a lesson there, I learned something new because they spoke about techniques in terms of word pictures that I could see and understand. I also liked that my instructors embraced ambiguity. I remember when I asked about the best line for moguls, whether I should go in the troughs, which seemed easiest, on top of the moguls, which seemed the coolest, or the uphill side of the troughs or the downhill side. The answer I got was "It depends" and then we talked for several chairlift rides about situations for choosing different places to turn on a mogul. I am so thankful for all the things I learned at Taos.

When I was at Taos, I noticed that the décor is different from most ski resorts. It has hints of the native-American sub-culture almost everywhere. It almost has an "I'm leaving the country" feeling in some places because the look, feel and vibe of restaurants, lodges, hotels, and bars can be so different from what I am used to. For those of you who enjoy experiencing different sub-cultures, I would put Taos at the top of your bucket list.

I also feel the need to mention art when I think about Taos. It seemed like Taos had more art galleries than any other ski town that comes to mind. Although my favorite art gallery is in Breckenridge, Colorado (it is probably my favorite because it has a lot of oil paintings), Taos art galleries offer vast varieties in style and form. It has been said that Taos has more artists per capita than any town in the world, including Paris. Although I'm not sure anyone has actually counted the artists, it does feel like a community that values art highly. It is also worth exploring the art in Santa Fe on the way to Taos; it's a cool town.

With all the art in New Mexico, it's hard to find time to get to all the ski resorts, but New Mexico has eight community mountains in addition to Taos that can be enjoyed if you are exploring the state.

NEW MEXICO RESORTS	LIFTS	TRAILS	SKIABLE ACRES
TAOS SKI VALLEY	14	72	1294
SKI APACHE	11	55	750
SKI SANTA FE	7	77	660
PAJARITO MOUNTAIN	6	40	300
RED RIVER SKI AREA	7	57	257
SIPAPU	5	41	200
SANDIA PEAK	5	31	200
SKI CLOUDCROFT	5	27	74
ANGEL FIRE RESORT	7	79	30

A friend told me about his vacation to New Mexico. He had been planning to ski one day at Taos. However, the road he needed to take was closed, so he skied at the Ski Santa Fe resort instead. He had a great day and was very glad for that experience.

Taos may be the only mountain in New Mexico big enough to be widely thought of as a destination ski resort, but there are other resorts that are good to know about.

Since there are many people who tend to set apart a week each year for a vacation to ski or snowboard, I will focus my comments in this book on the ski resorts that have at least 1,000 skiable acres. If you are going to ski the same mountain every day for six days in a row, one thousand acres provides enough variety to have every day be an adventure. However, I will at least provide a quick mention of every ski resort of every size for your awareness because you may want to consider going to smaller resorts as well.

Although I am writing this book especially for the people who take one or two ski vacations per year, if you ski more often, you will love this book even more. If you ski less than one week per year, this book can help you pick your dream resorts for those precious few vacations. This book can also be a happy escape from the everyday. It is fun to read and to think about the wonderfully different resorts. The adventures that can be had at each place are as varied as each snowflake that falls.

3. Montana's Wide Open Spaces

Montana's Wide Open Spaces make for amazing wide-open slopes.

Big Sky

Big Sky Resort is big. It has an all time large 5,800 skiable acres. Vail used to be the mountain with the most skiable acres until 2013 when Big Sky purchased a private ski area on Spirit Mountain and the adjacent Moonlight Basin Ski Area.

Interestingly, Big Sky is not marketing its skiable acres; it is marketing its elbow room. There are plenty of skiable acres per skier. Most of us have had that feeling of doing a run and not seeing another person on it; it's a cool feeling.

The numbers back up the elbow room advertising. Last year, Big Sky had only one-fifth the visitors as Vail. Picture a place that only has a small fraction of the skiers that are usually on the slopes with you. That is a pretty picture.

Another heart warming picture happens at Big Sky every year; the Turkey For a Ticket Food-Raiser. In the last 10 years, the event has collected about $200,000 pounds of food for local area food banks.

MONTANA RESORTS	LIFTS	TRAILS	SKIABLE ACRES
BIG SKY	29	300	5,800
WHITEFISH MOUNTAIN	14	105	3,000
BRIDGER BOWL	8	71	2,000
DISCOVERY	8	70	2,000
RED LODGE MOUNTAIN RESORT	7	70	1,700
GREAT DIVIDE	6	140	1,600
BLACKTAIL MOUNTAIN	4	25	1,000
LOST TRAIL POWDER MOUNTAIN	8	45	1,000
TURNER MOUNTAIN	1	25	1,000
MONTANA SNOWBOWL	4	37	950
SHOWDOWN	4	36	640
TETON PASS	3	39	330
MAVERICK MOUNTAIN	1	15	250

The state of Montana has many resorts that offer extensive wide open spaces without crowds. There are nine resorts with 1,000 or more skiable acres. If you like going off the beaten path, if you prefer a lot of room to maneuver your turns, or if you like wide open spaces, Montana ski resorts can bring you wide open smiles.

It's worth noticing the 1,600 skiable acres at Great Divide because that is a lot of acres for a resort that focuses on pleasing snowboarders.

With 4,350 feet of vertical drop, Big Sky has plenty of downhill action to enjoy. The longest run is six miles long; I think that might also be the record in the United States. With over 400 inches of annual snowfall, Big Sky is a big mountain that is worth visiting.

MONTANA RESORTS	FEET AT PEAK	FEET AT BASE	VERTICAL DROP	INCHES ANNUAL SNOWFALL
BIG SKY	11,160	6,800	4,350	400
TURNER MOUNTAIN	5,952	3,842	2,110	375
BRIDGER BOWL	8,700	6,100	2,600	350
WHITEFISH MOUNTAIN	6,816	4,464	2,352	335
LOST TRAIL POWDER	8,200	6,400	1,800	300
MONTANA SNOWBOWL	7,600	5,000	2,600	300
TETON PASS	7,200	6,189	1,010	300
BLACKTAIL MOUNTAIN	6,675	5,235	1,440	250
RED LODGE	9,416	7,016	2,400	250
SHOWDOWN	8,200	6,800	1,400	240
DISCOVERY	8,150	5,770	2,380	200
GREAT DIVIDE	7,329	5,750	1,580	150
MAVERICK MOUNTAIN	8,900	1,600	2,000	140

Seven resorts in Montana get over 300 inches of average annual snowfall. It's only a matter of time until some of these become more well known.

Turner Mountain

Turner Mountain gets 375 inches of annual snowfall. Ski Magazine said that Turner Mountain "might offer the best lift-assisted powder skiing in the U.S." With an accolade like that, from a source like Ski Magazine, none of us should neglect Turner. Interesting, while the mountain is known for it's good powder, the mountain grooms more than 50% of its runs.

Whitefish Mountain

Big Mountain was renamed Whitefish Mountain Resort in 2007. If I were an intermediate skier, Whitefish Mountain is where I would want to go. Whitefish's terrain difficulty is as follows: 12% Beginner, 40% Intermediate, 42% Advanced, 6% Expert. Forty percent of 3,000 skiable acres is a lot of acreage to enjoy. The mountain has great bowl and tree skiing, as well as five terrain parks and a skier/boarder cross course.

Bridger Bowl

Bridger Bowl in Bozeman, MT has 4 large bowls, 8 chairlifts, and a 2,500 square foot food and beverage facility with a soapstone fireplace and beautiful mountain views. The 2000 skiable acres receive about 350 inches of snow each year.

Discovery

Discovery has three faces. The front face has gently sloping runs and more advanced wide, groomed cruisers. Things step up a notch off the Granite chair, with steeper groomed runs and mogul skiing. The backside has steeper slopes. Discovery provides 20% beginner, 25% intermediate, 25% advanced, and 30% expert terrain. With more skiable acres than some of the well known mountains, it's a wonder that more people haven't discovered Discovery Mountain.

Red Lodge Mountain Resort

Red Lodge is a year-round resort. In 1994, Red Lodge Mountain purchased Red Lodge Golf Course. This 18-hole championship golf course made it possible for Red Lodge Mountain to become a year-round resort.

Great Divide

Great Divide is Montana's "terrain park place." This place provides almost 100 features in their parks. The features include rails, boxes, and snow features (like jumps) that are changed every week. There are six parks to ride. The fun does not have to stop early; five parks are open every Friday night until 9 PM so you can ride the features under the lights.

Lost Trail

Lost Trail Powder Mountain is a nice family mountain that sits atop the Continental Divide on Highway 93 where Montana and Idaho meet. There are always charming locals to talk with at Lost Trail. The people who ski and ride here enjoy the "old school" feel and never having to wait in a lift line.

Smaller Mountains

In Montana, the smaller mountains are Snowbowl, Showdown, Teton Pass and Maverick Mountain. I want to keep you aware of all of the ski mountains in each state because sometimes the smaller mountains have something special.

- Snowbowl is located in the western part of the state. It is 12 miles from Missoula, one of Montana's two University towns.
- I like Showdown's tagline "all natural since 1936." Showdown is Montana's oldest ski area. With over 75 years of renegade skiing and riding, Showdown has a personality to it. They talk about the "crazy awesome snow." It puts a smile on my face to think of this place.
- Teton Pass advertises "zero lift lines." It is located in the Lewis and Clark National Forest.
- Maverick Mountain is a non-commercial mom-and-pop ski mountain.

Fun can be had at any Montana Mountain. The next group of mountains to consider is in the state with plentiful powder, Utah.

4. Utah Powder

Most skiers and riders agree that Utah gets the best powder in the United States. The snow receives high accolades for both quantity and quality. It is dry, light and deep.

Utah uses the line, "greatest snow on earth," for good reason. The state receives, on average, 18 "monster dumps" in which 12 inches or more of snow falls within a 24-hour period, throughout the winter. Even more important when you are planning your ski vacation is that from December through March, more than a foot of snow falls every five days.

Alta

One of the most impressive reasons that people love Alta is that it averages about 560 inches of fresh snow per year. No other resort in Utah gets as much snow.

Some people say that Alta got its name from the word altitude. Alta is high up on the mountain, so in the spring when other mountains get a little rain, Alta is still getting snow. When other mountains warm up in the springtime and begin to melt, Alta's altitude keeps the temperatures cool enough to maintain the snow. Alta is the snowiest place in Utah.

Alta is one of the only skiers-only mountains left. (The others are Deer Valley and Mad River Glen.) Since I both ski and snowboard − why is that a good thing? The love of skiing runs deep at Alta. It's fun to be around other people who are passionate about skiing. Alta has a vibe all its own. It's not only that people there have an intense love for skiing; it's also the unique experience of being outdoors in such an unspoiled environment. Everything feels natural in Alta. There is a sense of exploration and adventure in undeveloped landscapes. It almost doesn't feel like a ski resort, it feels more like being outside in nature on skis.

There is a lot of natural terrain variation. Some resorts have mostly one type of terrain; Alta has it all. It is fun to venture beyond the most popular slopes, and to pass through the gates that appear throughout the mountain. The gates are openings in the roped off sections that lead to more challenging terrain (so don't pass through unless you are at least a solid intermediate skier).

Some of the gate openings lead uphill, but can be skated and sidestepped, with skis on, to get up the modest inclines. The thing I love most about the gates is that sometimes they are closed. For example, it recently snowed 22 inches in just a couple of days. During that massive downpour of snow, East Castle, Devil's Castle, and the back side of the mountain were closed due to avalanche danger. When the snowing subsided and a blue sky emerged, the powder on those slopes was still untouched. They opened one area each day. So I got five days of fresh tracks in a row. One of those days was my best day of the season and reminded me of the last time I went heli-skiing.

Alta has very loyal clientele. Many people come back to Alta, from all over the country, year after year. There are also many Salt Lake City locals who are passionate about the resort. Alta enthusiasts are not only loyal to the mountain; they are zealous.

More than any other mountain, Alta skiers are passionate enough about their mountain to put Alta stickers on their helmets, their skis and their gear. I have seen more Alta stickers than stickers from several other resorts combined. It doesn't stop there. A walk through the parking lot usually displays multiple cars with "Ski Utah" license plates and Alta license plate frames.

The Alta Historical Society is active and frequently has events that you can join. I went to an Alta Historical Society event that was hosted at the Alta Lodge. The audience laughed and laughed at the stories of Alta in the 60s. From the stories I heard, I gathered that although much has changed, the camaraderie at Alta remains the same.

People have many reasons for loving Alta. Some people feel safer in the skier-only environment. I've never seen any statistics on snowboarders being involved in more collisions, but I can tell you that there is a strong perception among the apprehensive that skiers have fewer collisions than snowboarders. I don't know whether this is fact or fiction, but for a scared skier, not seeing a snowboarder within collision range is calming. I'm glad that there is a mountain for the timid. Otherwise, they may stop skiing.

Many people also like that the areas at the top of the lifts are not congested with people because, in general, skiers vacate the lift area quickly. The anti-crowd people appreciate that there are no crowds to navigate through when they get off the lift.

When you go to Alta, it might be helpful to know that on the way there is sometimes a flashing sign that says that state law requires you have snow tires or carry chains in your vehicle between November 1 and May 1. If you decide to take the bus, the Utah Transit Authority bus ride is free between Alta and Snowbird. Dial 511 on a cell phone to get current Utah Road Conditions. The Utah Department of Transportation sometimes restricts travel on the canyon road, State Highway 210, for avalanche control.

Alta has free parking with access to the entire mountain. If you have beginner skiers in your group, need daycare, or plan to go to ski school, then the Albion Base parking lot at the end of the road is best. Although, all lifts and runs can be accessed from either parking lot, intermediate skiers and advanced skiers find it best to park in the first lot, which is the Wildcat Base parking lot. From there, they can ride the Collins lift to get to the Sugarloaf or Supreme lifts.

Alta is probably the best ski resort for an American to be a liftee at. Liftees at Alta get more ski time per day than most. Many of them live in ski-in/ski-out accommodations on the mountain. Many mountains focus their seasonal hiring in foreign countries, Alta has a lot of young people who grew up locally and love the mountain as much as the rest of us.

Lodge life is still alive and well at Alta. The Rustler Lodge is the most upscale. The Peruvian has the bar with the party scene. The Snowpine Lodge has delicious multi-course dinners. The Alta Lodge and the Goldminer's Daughter are most convenient to the Collins Chairlift.

Alta was the first resort that I ever went to that used RFID on their lift tickets. (Radio Frequency Identification is a technology that incorporates the use of electromagnetic or electrostatic coupling in the radio frequency portion of the electromagnetic spectrum to uniquely identify an object, animal or person). Although it is becoming more common for resorts to use RFID tickets, Alta was one of the first.

Both Alta and Snowbird offer a Boarding Pass program. The Boarding Pass program allows you to ski for half-price within 24 hours of arrival. There are requirements like pre-registration online at least 24 hours prior to your flight departure, and providing photo ID and flight boarding pass at any ticket window.

Even though Alta is a skiers-only mountain, snowboarders are allowed to join the Alta Snowcat tours. There are 375 Snowcat accessible acres at Alta.

Alta's closing day party was one of the best. Interestingly, it didn't involve a slush pond, like most mountains. Besides the bands in the parking lot for most of the day, the zealous partiers in original costumes entertained the crowd by launching off five different kinds of jumps. After the jumps, the crowd headed to the top of High Rustler to take in the view before finishing the day with more live music.

Before we move on from Alta, I'd like to let some friends tell a story about when they were skiing there. Brandon started, "We just got to Alta. We were all pumped up because there are about six inches of new powder. We were on the top of Sugarloaf chair and then we took the high line around the Sugarloaf chair, in order to not go underneath it where there is an intermediate area; we were trying to find some untracked powder. Since there wasn't that much open so early in the season, we went the highest traverse we could take around there just to get a few turns in the powder, six inches of powder; that was our idea.

"And so we come whipping around this traverse and we are moving along and there are four of us following each other and I'm in the lead. I'm looking down the hill. So I'm traversing and I'm looking down the hill to see which three turns I am going to take in the powder. All of a sudden – I never saw it – Whack! I'm gasping for air, upside down, fallen down in the snow."

Now Joshua continues the story, "So I am behind Brandon and I see Brandon go down, and I think that he must have hit a rock. Brandon wouldn't go down like that. So I'm looking at him and all of a sudden, something hits me, square in the sternum. Boom! And I go down and I'm gasping for air and I end up lying on top of him. And I look up and all of a sudden, Tyler comes along. He hits it with his shoulder and then there are three of us and then the next guy comes along and he stops. He hits it, but he stops. That little, tree with the top broken off was bending over to point straight at him."

Brandon said cheerfully, as if thinking about a fond memory, "My coat was torn. It broke my ribs. It was bad. Joshua's coat also ripped. He duck taped his coat, but mine was trashed, I had to get a new coat."

Joshua finishes the story, "Later we called up John. He was an extreme skier and he was going to come meet us the next day or the day after that and I told him the story. John shared the story with his wife. She visualized it and laughed. Then she asked, 'Who are you going skiing with, the three stooges?'

Those guys love Alta and they talk about it with happiness in their voices. They have been back again and again since then. Don't worry. The bent little tree is gone now. It is a very safe mountain. The story my friends told me demonstrates how the skiers at Alta are so passionate about skiing. They love skiing so much; every single story about skiing is told with jubilance. The love of skiing runs deep at Alta. There is something about skiing that is worth being fanatical about. There is nothing like the terrain, the powder or the vibe at Alta.

The passion for skiing at Alta may partially derive from the history of the town. Back in 1865, it was a mining town. In 1938, the first Collins lift was constructed out of pieces from an aerial mining tram. Alta was the second ski mountain in U.S. history to build a chairlift, right after Sun Valley and before the first chairlift was built in Europe. Alta played a major role in leading the way for ski resorts everywhere.

The skiers who ski at Alta are passionate about the mountain. They care more about their skiing experience than lifts or facilities. However, Alta is planning 12 projects for the mountain, including a tram to Mount Baldy and a new Wildcat Chairlift. The projects will provide additional uphill capacity, avalanche control, parking, additions to buildings, and environmental restoration.

Snowbird

I've skied both Snowbird and Alta in one day when I wanted to meet up with some friends who had Snowbird tickets. Even though the two resorts are owned by different companies, you can ski from one mountain to the other, if you buy the appropriate duel mountain pass. The two resorts have different vibes, different amenities, and sometimes different snow conditions. Together, the two resorts offer 4,700 skiable acres.

Snowbird and Alta are located just a few minutes apart by car, and seconds apart by skis. When you are coming from Salt Lake City, up highway 201, you will reach Snowbird first. If you keep going on that same road, you will get to Alta a couple of miles later.

More people stop at the first resort on Highway 201; Snowbird gets more skier visits than Alta. However, with 2500 skiable acres, the mountain is a little larger. Snowbird has uphill capacity for over 17,000 skiers and snowboarders per hour.

Snowbird is a great resort with nice amenities. The resort has many conveniences, including a fully staffed medical clinic and pharmacy on site, as well as a United States Post Office. For dining, Snowbird has 15 restaurants and eateries, serving everything from fine dining to burgers and beer.

Snowbird also offers conveniences for families. Camp Snowbird is a state-licensed, fully staffed child-care center, for children age six weeks to 12 years old, which offers full day and half-day programs.

Snowbird's Cliff Lodge is ski-in, ski-out. The Lodge at Snowbird, The Inn and The Iron Blosam Lodge are within walking distance of the tram and chairlifts. There is good reason to book at one of these lodges. Snowbird averages 500 inches of dry Utah powder annually. Some of the lodging for Snowbird that is not located at the base of the mountain is separated from the mountain by a road that is prone to occasionally be forced to close due to snow conditions and avalanche danger. This means that people in most communities have to wait for the snow to be cleared before they can travel to the mountain. It also means all the freshly fallen snow is enjoyed only by the people who are already at the resort.

Even with that said, Snowbird is, in some ways, the most accessible year-round resort in North America. The reason is that you can hop on an early flight and be on the slopes by noon that same day. Snowbird is less than 30 miles from Salt Lake City International Airport, which has more than 600 daily non-stop flights from most major U.S. cities. Snowbird is a 45-minute drive from the airport, making same-day flying and skiing a reality.

Flying and skiing in the same day is definitely an option at Snowbird; and so is skiing and golfing. With about 200 ski days each season, Snowbird provides Utah's longest ski season. It's usually mid-November through May, but some years, skiing continues all the way into July.

Snowbird is a relatively young resort; it opened in December of 1971. Its longest run is Chip's run which is 2.5 miles. Snowbird's longest descent is Gad Valley, a 3.5 mile descent.

Not many ski resorts in the United States have trams, so if you like to try all different kinds of things, then going to Snowbird to ride the tram is another thing to have on your list. The scenic aerial tram goes up to an 11,000-foot Peak. The ten-minute trip along a 1.6 mile cable and up 2,900 vertical feet provides a great sightseeing experience if you are near the window. In addition to the views, some people like the tram because groups of over 100 people get to the top at the same time and then there is a lag time with no one arriving at the top. Therefore, relaxed skiers can let the speedsters go by and then they have the runs all to themselves. The speedsters may be trying to beat the tram to the bottom. Some people like to race it, just for fun. I recommend getting the ticket that includes the tram, but it you want to save some money, there is usually a chairlift-only pass, which does not include the tram.

Snowbird has 1,000 acres for snowcat skiing. Proceeds from the Snowbird Snowcat Skiing for Nature program benefit the Cottonwood Canyons Foundation and the Wasatch Water Legacy Partnership.

Racers tend to like Snowbird for the long groomed runs. Snowbird also offers some of the best expert terrain in Utah.

UTAH RESORTS	MOST INTERMEDIATE AND STEEPER TERRAIN % BEG/INT/ADV/EXPERT
PARK CITY	8/52/31/0
EAGLE POINT	20/35/45/0
SNOW BASIN	20/50/15/15
SOLITUDE	20/50/30/0
BRIGHTON	21/39/40/0
ALTA	25/40/35/0
POWDER MOUNTAIN	25/40/35/0
SNOWBIRD	27/38/20/15
DEER VALLEY	27/41/27/5

UTAH RESORTS	MOST BEGINNER TERRAIN BY PERCENT OF TERRAIN BEG/INT/ADV/EXPERT
BRIAN HEAD	30/35/30/0
NORDIC VALLEY	30/40/30/0
CHERRY PEAK	30/45/25/0
BEAVER MOUNTAIN	35/40/25/0
SUNDANCE RESORT	35/45/20/0

Beaver Mountain and Sundance Resort have the high percentages of beginner terrain. Finding beginner terrain in Utah is usually relatively easy because many resorts in Utah have high percentages of intermediate terrain.

If you know how to ski deep snow, then it is good to know that Snowbird, Brighten, Solitude and Powder Mountain all receive about 500 inches of snow most years. It's even better to know that Alta gets the most snow with an average of 560 inches each year.

UTAH RESORTS	FEET AT PEAK	FEET AT BASE	VERTICAL DROP	THE MOST AVERAGE ANNUAL SNOWFALL IN INCHES
ALTA	10,550	8,530	2,020	560
BRIGHTON	10,500	8,755	1,745	500
POWDER	9,422	6,900	3,399	500
SNOWBIRD	11,000	7,760	3,240	500
SOLITUDE	10,035	7,988	2,047	500

UTAH RESORTS	FEET AT PEAK	FEET AT BASE	VERTICAL DROP	AVERAGE ANNUAL SNOWFALL IN INCHES
EAGLE POINT	10,500	9,100	1,500	450
BEAVER	8,800	7,200	1,600	400
BRIAN HEAD	10,920	9,600	1,320	370
PARK CITY	10,000	6,800	3,200	358
CHERRY PEAK	7,050	5,775	1,265	322
DEER VALLEY	9,570	6,570	3,000	300
NORDIC VALLEY	6,400	5,400	1,000	300
SNOW BASIN	9,350	6,400	2,950	300
SUNDANCE	8,250	6,100	2,150	300

Solitude

The first time I went to Solitude, there was too much snow for my skill level and my skis, so I left and went back to Colorado. Not many skiers leave a resort because of too much snow, but it can happen in Utah. Knowing what I know now, the first thing I should have done when I found myself sinking into hip high powder is I should have gone to the ski shop to rent some wider skis. When in deep powder, it is possible to sink to the bottom if one's skis are not wide enough. The next thing I should have done is gotten a lesson. There are techniques to help skiers float on top of deep snow. Some people think of leaning back a little. Personally, I now think of keeping my feet a little forward of my usual stance. Some people swing their arms a little. Some skiers put more even weight between their uphill and downhill ski than usual. These are just some of the techniques skiers talk about. If you find yourself in powder that is too deep to ski, it is certainly a time when the price of the lesson is well worth the smiles the snow will bring you.

The last time I went to Solitude, I had just finished skiing several days at a more rustic resort, which made me appreciate Solitude's excellent quality and amenities all the more. I had been told about the car valet service over the phone, so I pulled up as close to the building as I could get and immediately there was someone there to meet me to take my luggage. However, it wasn't until I traveled up the elevator and opened the door to my room that a huge smile overtook my face. Without thinking, I breathed out any tenseness from the last few days of challenges. I still was smiling as I collapsed into a chair knowing that I was going to be very comfortable here. Then I opened the glass door facing the mountain and took in the view of the mountain. It was then that I knew my vacation had officially started. There is something about the "otherness" of vacations that refresh and restore my soul.

The next morning, I was not disappointed by the snow. Since I had been skiing in the area, I knew the general conditions to expect, but Solitude was a step above expectations. I attribute the better than average snow to the lack of crowds at Solitude. The snow lasts much longer when fewer people are skiing it. In fact, I never waited in a lift line when I was there early season.

My favorite restaurant at Solitude was Honeycomb Grill. I found myself alternating between trying a new place and going back to the Honeycomb. I recommend The Roundhouse (the restaurant on the slopes, located between the Moonbeam and Eagle Express chairlifts) for people who like variety in their eating experiences. The Roundhouse features Himalayan and Wasatch-inspired mountain food. If you like to try new dishes, perhaps there is something on this list that you have never had before: Bear River spinach shepherd's pie, Utah funeral potatoes, lamb curry, chicken makhani, saag paneer, dahl baht, thukpa, onion bhaji and naan.

The quaint village provided enough shops for the few days I was there. Despite the name, Solitude is very inviting. Its charming, European-style village has fun activities like ice skating, snowshoeing and making s'mores by one of the fire pits. I also enjoyed Club Solitude where I borrowed some magazines. The club also had books, DVDs, board games and an Xbox, in addition to saunas, a heated pool and hot tubs.

Brighton

Brighton is Utah's only resort that can boast that 100% of its terrain is accessible by high-speed quads. High speed quads are wonderful in and of themselves, so that we can ski more runs in a day. The high speed quads at Brighton are especially great because it may be the only mountain where families can ride together on the same lift and then peel off onto different trails – beginner, intermediate, or expert – and all meet at the bottom to ride the lift together again.

Brighton does a lot of grooming to cater to the large number of snowboarders:

- ✓ All beginner runs are groomed nightly
- ✓ Almost all intermediate trails are groomed nightly
- ✓ Although the main runs are groomed, the terrain for experts is usually left natural for skiers and riders who like their powder deep.

Brighton is a great place for snowboarders and a great place for teenagers. The majority of people at Brighton when I was there were in their mid to late teens. This creates a vibrant atmosphere. The kids are enthusiastic about life and riding. For the most part, the rebellious teenagers are not there.

Brighton attracts teenagers who are passionate about snowboarding and the camaraderie they have with their friends.

The first thing I noticed about the mountain was how large one of the areas at the top of the lift is; there is ample room for snowboarders to strap in.

The nicest thing about riding at Brighton is that I never got stuck anywhere. There was always at least a gentle pitch to keep me moving down the mountain. I love that riding is so easy at Brighton.

It's also easy to find something good to eat. I'm still thinking about that Alpine burger I had for lunch. It was delicious. It was a cheeseburger with onion rings on top and barbecue sauce on the side.

The liftees are friendly and the ticket staff is helpful. In all, it's an upbeat, happy place to be. The place to go after skiing for apres is the Green Ally. It's fun to tell the tales of the day there.

The last time I skied Brighton, I stayed at the ski-in, ski-out Brighton Lodge. The convenience is a great attribute of that lodge. Another thing I appreciated there was the tall tree right outside the window. The trees are close to the building, which gives an immersed in nature feeling, even from the inside of the building.

Although most riders stay on the groomed trails, there are trees and chutes, cliffs and natural terrain parks all within bounds for those who like "white knuckle" terrain. Brighton has four terrain parks for all abilities. Although the features in the terrain park are constantly changing, there is usually a half pipe to ride.

You will most likely hear about Brighton from your friends. The mountain doesn't do much advertising. It's a low-key place and there are plenty of picnic tables for BYO lunches. A nice amenity is that there are computer plug-ins in

Alpine Rose cafeteria, so you can email friends to tell them how much fun you are having. If you have kids, then bring them because at Brighton, kids seven years old and under ski and ride free.

Brighton is well known for its ski and snowboard school because of its devotion to students' progress. It is "the place where Utah learns to ski and ride and keeps on learning." Brighton's Ski and Snowboard School has private lessons, daily group classes for every ability level of skiers and riders, and specialty series for kids, women, and seniors. The school has over 175 instructors.

Brighton also has the most night skiing terrain in Utah with 22 runs on over 200 lighted acres. The mountain is open 9 AM – 9 PM, so ski as long as you can.

Park City Mountain Resort

Park City Mountain is now the country's largest ski area, with more than 7,300 skiable acres between the original Park City Mountain Resort and the added Canyons Village terrain. (Before the two resorts were combined, Park City had 3,300 skiable acres and the Canyons Resort had 4,000 skiable acres.) The Canyons Resort used to be the largest ski area in Utah, now it is part of the largest ski resort in the country.

Compared to other large ski resorts, Park City wins the size award by a large margin. Colorado's Vail resort has over 5,000 skiable acres and Montana's Big Sky has almost 6,000 skiable acres. Park City is now the largest by over a thousand skiable acres.

The resort completed its $50 million capital improvement program that included the Quicksilver Gondola and the Miner's Camp restaurant. The Quicksilver Gondola is extremely useful for intermediates and experts to get from Park City to Canyons Village and vice versa (because of the blue terrain on the Canyons side of the gondola, the resort recommends that guests are at elast an intermediate level skier or snowboarder). The Quicksilver Gondola takes 9 minutes from one side to the other.

If you like to plan your ski day, you can download the free EpicMix app onto any Apple or Android phone. The EpicMix Maps feature displays where you are on mountain to help navigate from lift to lift. In addition, the app also shows wait times for chairlifts or gondolas in real time.

If you prefer to ski whatever is in front of you, don't worry about ending up on the wrong side of the resort at the end of the day. It's good to know that if you end up at the wrong base area, Park City has free and convenient public transportation. Park City Mountain Base area and Canyons Village both have major transit hubs at either side of the resort. The Park City Base area transit hub is in front of the main parking lots. The Canyons Village transit hub is next to The Cabriolet. The most convenient bus route between the two resorts is called "Lime Canyons".

The Canyons has always been a great place for groups, weddings, and for anytime 15,000 square feet of meeting space are needed. Over 100 restaurants and bars are within minutes of the area.

The first time I went to the Canyons, I parked in the designated parking lot and took the Cabriolet up to the main area of the mountain. The Cabriolet is like a gondola, but it is not enclosed. I was going up in the springtime for an afternoon concert. The air was crisp and the view was beautiful. The stage was set up not far from the top of the Cabriolet. It's a great environment for a concert because people have several choices: standing up front near the stage, sitting in the middle on lawn chaises provide by the Canyons resort, in the back at tables at the Umbrella Bar, on the side surrounding a fire pit, and on the other side where stores, including places to get picnic food and beverages, were nearby.

I recommend Park City if you are celebrating anything. My birthday was last week and I chose Park City to ski on that day. We then visited art galleries, heard live music and had a delicious dinner at a restaurant with wonderful ambiance. There are also fun bars there. No matter what you are celebrating: a birthday, an engagement, an anniversary, a promotion… Park City is a celebratory place that will add enjoyment to your festivities.

The Park City Mountain Resort is also a good mountain for people who like long runs; "homerun" is 3.5 miles long.

UTAH RESORTS	LIFTS	TRAILS	SKIABLE ACRES
PARK CITY	41	300	7,300
POWDER MOUNTAIN	7	154	3,800
SNOW BASIN	10	104	3,300
SNOWBIRD	13	168	2,500
ALTA	10	116	2,200
DEER VALLEY	21	101	2,026
SOLITUDE	8	65	1,200
BRIGHTON	6	62	1,050
BEAVER	4	48	828
BRIAN HEAD	9	71	665
EAGLE POINT	5	39	600
SUNDANCE	5	42	450
CHERRY PEAK	4	20	200
NORDIC VALLEY	4	22	110

Deer Valley

Who doesn't like to be pampered? Deer Valley lives and breathes customer service and amenities. The resort is consistently ranked #1 in guest service and they deliver an unmatched customer experience. Deer Valley makes an art out of caring for guests' needs. They offer first-class amenities such as uniformed ski valets, groomed-to-perfection slopes, and award-winning cuisine. Deer Valley revolutionized ski area service and they provide a level of care rarely found.

In addition to service, Deer Valley is known for its exquisitely groomed cruising trails. Deer Valley's ability to expertly lay carpets of corduroy is unsurpassed. Those manicured trails provide exceptional carving surfaces. However, among its six peaks, the mountain also has nicely spaced trees, as well as bumps, chutes and bowls.

The lodges in Deer Valley have a sophisticated style. To get around, there are complimentary in-town shuttles provided by Cadillac. The dining is superb.

Deer Valley is perfect for people who are used to the best of everything (or who would like to become used to the best of everything).

The first time I went to Deer Valley, I summarized my favorite attributes about this mountain as lifts, lunch, and lines in the moguls. There are chairlifts all over the mountain. It is so pleasant to not have to traverse because there are so many lifts. It may be because I had just spent weeks skiing a mountain that doesn't have many chairlifts, but I really appreciated how the large number of chairlifts at the resort give perfect access to all parts of the mountain. There is no need for long traverses at Deer Valley.

At lunchtime, I was happily surprised. I had heard about the food at Deer Valley, so I expected it to be excellent, but it was beyond that. I loved that there was a carving station, so I was able to get a Thanksgiving themed meal of turkey, mixed vegetables, potatoes, gravy and cranberry chutney in about two minutes. Walking into Silver Lake Lodge and getting food that quickly was a surprise. The price was also a pleasant surprise; the food was an excellent value. It was delicious. To have a meal that good, during a break from skiing hard, is a delight.

All that being said, my favorite thing about Deer Valley was the mogul runs. I had heard from a ski buddy that many Deer Valley visitors stay on the groomers because the grooming is the best in the United States. It makes sense to stay on the groomers when you are at the best place for groomed runs. However, there are some of us who love moguls so much that we don't like to take too many runs without doing some bump runs. What this creates is an environment where only true bump skiers spend much time on the mogul runs. The skill level of these bump skiers create tight moguls with perfect lines.

Deer Valley is one of the three skier-only mountains left in the United States. The skier-only clientele creates better-shaped moguls. I will travel farther, and pay more money, in order to have better shaped moguls. The way snowboards push the snow when they turn is different than the way skis push the snow. Since moguls are formed by people pushing the snow when they turn, the moguls at Deer Valley are better because only skiers go through them.

Lastly, I want to mention the people at Deer Valley. The types of people who choose to ski Deer Valley are a pleasure to be around. The people are not only interesting to talk with, they are also both polite and kind. Deer Valley attracts people with high standards and high ideals.

The last time I was at Deer Valley, I broke a binding while skiing. My skiing buddy was ahead of me, so I texted him and asked him to take the chairlift up, so that he could lap me and then help me by carrying my ski down the mountain. No sooner than I hit send on the text, a fellow skier stopped to ask me if I needed help. I suppose he hadn't seen me ski because at first he thought I had one ski off because it was a steep section and that I just needed to get down to the milder slope in order to put my ski back on. When I showed him how my binding had separated from my ski, he offered to carry my ski without a binding down to the lift for me. He thought it would make it easier for me to walk down if I didn't have to carry the ski. He then skied away with my ski, enabling me to have an easier time balancing as I skied on one ski down the mountain. When I got to the bottom, the ski was exactly where he said he would leave it.

After I picked up the ski, I saw a safety patroller skiing into the lift area with his stretcher behind him. I asked him whether there would be a repair shop at the top of this lift, or whether there was a way for me to ski down farther to get to the bottom. He said, "Oh, you are the person without a ski, I was looking for you." When he saw that I clearly didn't need a stretcher, he used his radio to summon a snowmobile ride for me. The snowmobiler would take me directly to the village that had two repair shops.

My ski buddy then skied up to us and I recounted the story. The patroller gave him directions on where I was being taken and how he could meet me there by taking the lift up and then skiing the appropriate trails down.

The snowmobiler then arrived, and with Deer Valley style politeness, he courteously introduced himself and secured my skis and poles to the snowmobile. I enjoyed the ride.

One of the things that I thought about on the ride was how kind the people were. A skier took time away from his skiing to carry my ski for me. Someone who saw me from the chairlift alerted a liftee to call ski patrol. Ski patrol was assertive to help me. The snowmobiler was courteous. I felt like kindness was showered on me.

When I got to the repair area inside the Christy Sports Ski Shop, I talked with someone who was extremely knowledgeable, which was exactly what I was hoping for in that moment. He had the part that was broken on my binding. I felt relieved to leave my ski and broken binding in his hands while I went to lunch. He was kind, capable and sympathetic.

When I had finished lunch I went back to Christy Sports and my binding was repaired. Not only that, he had checked my other ski and saw that it was also about to go and he fixed that as well, as a courtesy. I left the shop feeling confident that he had done an excellent job.

I sometimes think that my safety is partially based on my skiing ability and my choices, and is occasionally based on my equipment. When I snapped into my binding, I knew it felt secure. When I gave it a test run on an intermediate slope, I knew the ski was reacting better than it had been handling that morning. I smiled at the thought of how fortunate I was that the Christy Sports repairperson was that good at what he does. I was thankful for his skills! Then I headed for the slopes that I love and my afternoon was consumed with fun.

Powder Mountain

Powder Mountain is something else. It's hard to put a size to it. Lifts serve 2,800 acres; the Powder Country Shuttle serves 1,200 acres. Lightening Ridge Snowcat Ride serves 700 acres. The Backcountry tour area, which is serviced by Snowcat Powder Safari and DMI/Wolf Canyon Tours, can access 3,000 and 1,000 acres respectively. In total, Powder Mountain has over 7,000 skiable acres. This is the most acres in any resort in the United States. The only reason Powder Mountain doesn't receive the accolades for the largest resort, is that it is not all accessible by chairlifts. (The cat-skiing tour acres do not count when comparing resorts.) Nevertheless, this is one large resort.

If you want to try snowcat skiing for the first time, I recommend doing it at Powder Mountain because they have a single ride that can be purchased for under $20. They also offer a sunset expedition for about $75. If you are not sure what a snowcat is, think part bulldozer, part snowmobile. It is a large truck-like vehicle on tracks that is designed to easily move on snow.

Half day Snowcat tours usually cost more than $300. There are over 4,200 acres of Snowcat accessible terrain at Powder Mountain. That is the most Snowcat accessible acres that I know of in the United States.

Some people think that due to improvements in technology, cat skiing can now almost rival heli-skiing in terms of both the quality and quantity of skiing it provides. The new snowcats are much better climbers than they used to be. This means that they can get up steeper grades and access much more terrain. Even the rides have become much more enjoyable as the cats drive much more smoothly and quietly than they used to.

Snowbasin

Snowbasin is a large, family friendly mountain. Kids as young as three years old can learn to snowboard. The ski school uses terrain-based learning in a dinosaur-themed environment. Kids can learn all the basics of snowboarding while riding over mellow terrain features like berms, rollers and rails. Snowbasin has four terrain parks with over 65 rails. The mountain's features progress gradually in difficulty, so snowboarders can be happy at this mountain for many years to come.

The mountain also has a four-lane tubing hill and 26 km of Nordic skiing trails.

Other Utah Ski Resorts

The smaller mountains in Utah, in terms of skiable acres, are: Beaver Mountain, Brian Head, Eagle Point, Sundance, Nordic Valley and Cherry Peak.

For those of you who are old-timers and are wondering about Wolf Mountain… Wolf Mountain is now called Nordic Valley.

Cherry Peak is the newest mountain in Utah. It opened during the 2015-2016 season. It's amazing to me that the Chadwick and Daimes families decided to create a brand new ski mountain. I love it when people pursue their dreams and use their passion for the good of their community.

Cherry Peak is private land that the Chadwick and Daimes families used to ski (only themselves) using their family's snowmobiles and by skinning up hill. Their family has owned the land since 1960.

When the family decided to open their land to the public for skiing, they wasted no time getting three triple chairlifts and a magic carpet installed. They have over 20 runs plus a terrain park, snow making capabilities, and a tubing hill. It is located seven minutes from downtown Richmond, Utah. I would like to support them next season. It might not be easy to create a brand new ski resort, but it is admirable. I hope they do well.

To summarize this chapter, Utah is a great place for ski mountains. Zrankings, who ranks "true snowfall" rates Utah ski resorts Alta, Snowbird, and Brighton in the top five most "true snowfall" mountains. Since Powder King in British Columbia and Grand Targhee in Wyoming are the other two resorts in the top five places with the most "true snowfall", let's travel to Wyoming. The next chapter will tell you about Wyoming ski resorts.

5. Technically Challenging Wyoming

Jackson Hole

Wyoming's most famous ski resort is Jackson Hole. The thing that I love most about Jackson Hole is that it is a ski vacation destination, unlike most ski vacation destinations. When I went there, I felt like the place has a unique culture because almost everyone was on vacation, which meant that almost everyone was exceptionally happy and exceptionally friendly. The nice thing about Jackson Hole not being as easy to travel to as some other mountains, is that it brings in happy vacationers whose enthusiasm for the mountain, for each other, and enjoying life is notable. There is no huge nearby city to bring in large numbers of stressed city dwellers. To be in a place filled with happy, hard-core skiers who are on vacation, is radical.

One of the many factors that cause the destination vacation skiers and riders to be so happy is the continuous improvement at Jackson Hole. The resort has invested over $100 million during the last 25 years in capital improvements.

Jackson Hole is technically challenging. It is famous worldwide for its huge 4,139 feet of vertical and unparalleled backcountry access. This resort has the longest and steepest vertical slope in the United States. Jackson Hole has 2,500 acres of legendary inbound terrain. The most famous run is Corbet's Couloir.

Some friends told me a story about Corbet's Couloir. Joshua started the story, "I'm in Jackson Hole. I was with a group of friends skiing. So I was with a group of friends, and

I'm working up the courage to go off Corbet's Couloir. And I'm standing there on the edge and there are a bunch of people who are also standing there, kind of doing the same thing as me… working up the courage while watching people try to ski it, and all of a sudden a guy comes out of nowhere, like at 30 miles per hour. Without stopping, he goes flying off the… It's kind of hard to describe… there is a little bit of a curve and there is a promontory after that."

Mike added, "Yeah, you've got to curve to the right after that."

Brandon remarked, "He went skiers left. Skiers left? Can you believe it?"

Joshua said, "He went to outer space. I think his skis and poles came off before he hit the snow. The guy had to be as high as a kite."

Brandon chimed in, "He lost his equipment before he landed. It was off and his arms and legs were flying and he had his buddy on the other promontory on the other side, taking a picture. I saw it. I was there before Joshua apparently because I saw the guy set up. He came down. I skied behind him on the way down, under the tram. Yeah, I saw these kids and they weren't good skiers. I thought they were obviously just going to take a look. And his buddy sets up on the other promontory with a camera and this guy walks back up and the he does this maneuver. He goes flying off. It was unreal."

Joshua finished with, "So I tell Brandon this story like 15 years later and Brandon goes, 'I was there.' We did not know each other back then, but we put the dates together and sure enough he was there."

They both saw the same thing at the same time in Jackson Hole when they didn't know each other, and now they are good friends. That's odd. It's not only a small world, it's a world that brings like-minded and skiing compatible people together.

Jackson Hole has the most vertical drop in Wyoming. Grand Targhee also has substantial vertical drop.

WYOMING RESORTS	FEET AT PEAK	FEET AT BASE	VERTICAL DROP
JACKSON HOLE	10,450	6,311	4,139
GRAND TARGHEE	9,920	7,851	2,270
PINECREEK	8,200	6,875	1,325
BEARTOOTH BASIN	10,900	9,900	1,000
WHITE PINE	9,500	8,400	1,100
SNOW KING	7,808	6,237	1,571
MEADOWLARK SKI LODGE	9,500	8,500	1,000
SNOWY RANGE	9,663	8,798	990
SLEEPING GIANT	7,400	6,600	800
HOGADON	8,000	7,400	600

Grand Targhee

Grand Targhee Resort is a year-round mountain resort. Although it is located on the western slope of the Tetons in Alta, Wyoming, it is accessible only through Teton Valley, Idaho. Because of the location 45 miles west of Jackson, some skiers ski both Jackson Hole and Grand Targhee in the same trip. Grand Targhee is known for epic powder days and family feel.

If you want to ski the Teton mountain range at a relaxed pace, Grand Targhee is a great place to go. There are wide-open spaces and plenty of powder to enjoy. The slower paced vibe at Grand Targhee is especially helpful for new skiers and family skiers.

In addition to the usual range of activities like snow shoeing, tubing, Nordic skiing and massage services, Grand

Targhee also offers an arcade, avalanche dog demos and evening snowcat tours.

Forbes Magazine has had Grand Targhee on their list of Top 10 ski Resorts. Ski Magazine has rated Grand Targhee in the top 2 resorts for best snow. ZRankings believes Grand Targhee is in the top 4 ski resorts for "best places to ski in March".

Jackson Hole and Grand Targhee have the most skiable acres in Wyoming.

WYOMING RESORTS	LIFTS	TRAILS	SKIABLE ACRES
JACKSON HOLE	12	80	2,500
GRAND TARGHEE	5	72	2,402
PINECREEK	2	30	640
BEARTOOTH BASIN	2	9	600
WHITE PINE	2	25	370
SNOW KING	5	24	350
MEADOWLARK SKI LODGE	3	14	300
SNOWY RANGE	5	29	250
SLEEPING GIANT	3	49	184
HOGADON	3	24	60

Although several mountains in Wyoming have less than 700 skiable acres, many of them are great places to learn to ski and ride. It can also be fun to go to some of the smaller resorts for a change of pace.

Pinecreek

If you go to the western part of Wyoming, there is Pinecreek ski area located in Cokeville that offers "skiing like it used to be". Pinecreek Mountain has 30 runs, over 1300 vertical feet, and a quad chairlift.

Beartooth Basin

Formerly called The Red Lodge International Ski and Snowboard Camp, Beartooth Basin is one of North America's oldest alpine ski training areas. When the previous ski camp owners aged, and the younger generation took over, the younger generation opened the area to the public and expanded its customers beyond the private groups and teams that had been the tradition in the past. There is no lodge, so it is a little bit like backcountry skiing with a lift.

White Pine

There is plenty of beginner terrain at White Pine. There is also a maze of cross-country trails.

Snow King

Snow King is near Jackson Hole. Snow King has lots of steep, expert terrain at an affordable price. If skiing isn't the only thing on your calendar for the day, this resort offers two-hour lift tickets at a great price. This resort also offers night skiing and snow tubing.

Meadowlark Ski Lodge

Meadowlark Ski Lodge is one of the ski areas in the Big Horn Mountains. It offers 300 skiable acres.

Antelope Butte

Antelope Butte is currently closed, but is raising funds to re-open. If you would like to donate so that the mountain can re-open that ski area in the Big Horn National Forest, you can donate online at this website: antelopebuttefoundation.org.

Snowy

Snowy Range Ski and Recreation Area offers a few short, steep runs and plenty of beginner terrain. It is located in in the southeast part of the state.

Sleeping Giant

Sleeping Giant Ski Area is one of America's oldest ski areas. It is located in Cody, Wyoming, and is only three miles from Yellowstone National Park.

Hogadon

Hogadon is located 15 minutes from downtown Casper, Wyoming. It's a relatively small resort with 60 acres and a vertical of 600 feet. This resort also offers 42 km of groomed cross-country trails.

To summarize Wyoming resorts, they offer some of the most technically challenging terrain, some of the happiest vacation spots, and deep powder. What more could you ask for! With all that, why are some Colorado mountains more famous?

6. The Famous Mountains

The famous mountains are in Colorado, and they are famous for good reason. What is similar about them, and what is different about them? What makes them so special compared to other mountains in their home state of Colorado? Why are the Colorado Mountains seemingly more famous than those in Utah, California, Wyoming, Idaho, or Canada? Is that changing? Why do some movie stars pick Telluride and others pick Aspen?

All mountains are different; all have their pros and cons. All mountains offer different mixes of strengths and weaknesses. Let's explore each mountain. The most famous mountains are Vail and Aspen.

Vail

Vail locals describe it as "like no place on earth," and there are a lot of people who think it is the best place on earth. There are many reasons to love this resort. There are many flights into Denver, non-stops from many locations, and Vail is almost the closest mountain to Denver airport. Loveland Ski resort and Keystone resort are both actually closer to Denver airport. Loveland and Keystone are both worth skiing and I'll tell you more about those resorts later, but for the people who like to experience the famous spots, Vail has to be at the top of the list.

Vail is known for its back bowls. Going to Vail and not going to the back bowls would be like going to Manhattan and not taking in a play on Broadway. You can do it and have a fantastic time, but you would be missing out on experiencing something truly special.

The feeling in the back bowls is euphoric. There is wide-open space, with snow everywhere. Other mountains have bowls, but none like Vail. If you happen to be back there on a powder day, the feeling is almost surreal, like floating downhill in slow motion. If you are there on a blue bird day, pure joy and exuberance will likely break out. A mere chairlift has transported you to another space and time. There are no problems or complications in the back bowls. There is only what is right before you, and it is very good.

For those of you who have never been in a bowl, imagine if you were miniaturized and left at the top of a cereal bowl. You might have a hard time getting down. The back bowls of Vail are not meant for beginner skiers. If you can call yourself at least an intermediate skier, a foretaste of heaven is waiting for you in the back bowls. If you can ski expert terrain, hello happy times.

The bowls are not the only fun to be had on this mountain. There is a lot of terrain and you can find just about any type of terrain that you want. Moguls, groomed, tree skiing; it's all there. More so than most mountains, it is easy to feel a sense of exploration at Vail. The mountain is so big and the terrain so varied that each run feels like exploring the unknown and finding precious jewels. Some of the finds are so good that you don't want to tell anyone about them, except your very closest friends. So we do that line again and again because we want to experience it as many times as possible in case, one day, word gets out and a gold rush ensues.

After skiing, the villages in Vail are wonderful. So many restaurants, so much shopping, après venues abound. Enjoying après-ski celebrations at a venue with outdoor seating is a favorite pastime of many visitors.

This famous mountain has more international visitors than any other U.S. resort that I know of. This melting pot of ski and snowboard enthusiasts from all over the world can make you feel like you left the country and went somewhere exotic. This may mean that you are less likely to turn that beautiful person you met from Europe or South America into a lasting relationship, but it can make for more interesting conversations.

For those of you who enjoy getting acquainted with people from other countries and cultures, Vail is the educational and relational experience to feast in.

The Aspen Snowmass Resort

It is clear to see why people love Vail, but why do people love Aspen? There are a variety of reasons.

If you have access to your own or a shared, private jet, Aspen is likely to be your top choice. In Aspen, there is a community of wealthy and famous people. If the wealth at the Sun Valley resort in Idaho is said to be "down to earth" wealth, and the wealth in Telluride can be creative and private, the wealth in Aspen may be the most flamboyant. Everything is relative and in Aspen, even a millionaire might feel middle class. So the culture here is very rich.

I've seen more Blockbuster actors, Disney channel actors, music Hall of Fame inductees and Fortune 500 CEOs in Aspen than at any other resort. To have a place where the ultra wealthy can socialize with their peers is a haven for some and the place that feels most like home for others. If you are ultra wealthy, you most likely know several people with homes in Aspen and if your friends are there, you may want to consider getting a place there yourself.

There are not only great friends to be made for the wealthy in Aspen, there are delectable meals to be enjoyed. Foodies love the town for the exceptional food experiences that it provides. The food culture is very strong. There are food and wine festivals throughout the year that encourage the ongoing enjoyment of food and the creation of new food experiences.

There are many restaurants in Aspen that make the trip there worth the journey. There are restaurants in many different styles of cuisine and many different price points. So even average American foodies go out of their way to make it to Aspen to enjoy the culinary experiences.

Let's talk about the skiing in Aspen. The resort is unique in that people who visit Aspen can ski four very different mountains. The mountains are not connected, so although it is humanly possible to ski all four mountains in one day, most people pick a mountain for the day and then ski another mountain the next day. The most well known is Aspen mountain, known among long-term locals as "Ajax." Aspen Mountain has everything you would expect in a mountain.

Aspen Mountain

I lived at the base of Aspen Mountain for a few months and I enjoyed being able to live in a real town with lots of stores and restaurants where I could walk to the food store and walk to lifts. The layout of Aspen has a classic American town feel.

The lodge at the top of the mountain has a lot of glass and beautiful views. The mid-mountain lodge has delicious pancakes and sandwiches. Ajax tavern at the base of the mountain is the go-to place for après on the mountain.

The skiing is solid. If it's good enough for Arnold Schwarzenegger's vacation, it's good enough for me. (Yes, I did see him on the slopes.)

Here is a story that my friend Joshua told about who he met on the mountain:

"I'm in Aspen with some friends and I'm skiing down an elevator shaft and I'm ahead of this other guy who I was with, and I ski down and I stop, and I'm waiting, and this girl, a very attractive girl, with a cute outfit skies down. She's a good skier. She comes down through the bumps and she skis up to me and she goes, 'There is some really good air down there', and she goes, 'I'll show you.' So she goes down and takes this cute little jump. And I'm like 'I'm going to fly, I'm going to fly'. The hormones are pumping. I go whipping down and she took the jump to the right and I figured the lip looks a little bigger on the left. It's blind after that but I figured, what the heck; it's got to be OK; there's got to be something down there. So I go flying down there. I lift off this lip and I look down and there are only rocks underneath me, and there is nowhere to land. I end up going in tips first, tips, top of my head, tips, top of my head, like four times. I end up miraculously not killing myself. Missing the rocks, I end up right at her feet. I am literally on my back, looking up at her. She looks down at me and she says, 'That's the most amazing thing I have ever seen in my life', and she skis away.

"I have my skis broken in half. I get no phone number, and she's gone. I never see her again. My skis busted. I have to walk down. And nothing. And I'm imagining she is seeing her friends after skiing going, 'I can't believe what I got this guy to do.' "

My experience in Aspen was different. The person that I love to follow down the mountain is David Peszek. Most people in Aspen call him Pez. He is the most technically correct skier that I have ever seen on the slopes. His turns are smooth beyond belief. I am a better skier from having skied behind him and seen the technical precision he demonstrates. He has been a racing coach, so if you like to go fast, he can give you some performance enhancing pointers. As time permits, he instructs on all terrain (Alpinetrainer@gmail.com).

Snowmass Mountain

A short bus ride away is Snowmass Mountain. I like it because it feels bigger. It has more groomers, more mogul runs, and more trails than I could ski in a single day. There is also some exceptional hike-to terrain at Snowmass. Some of it is inbounds and some of it is out of bounds. There are signs that clearly mark the out of bounds terrain where a beacon, shovel and probe are essential gear. However, if you prefer the safety of staying inbounds, there are plenty of off the beaten path areas that you can hike to. With 3,332 skiable acres, Snowmass has more skiable acres than any other resort in Colorado, except Vail, which has over 5,000 skiable acres.

Aspen Highlands

Aspen Highlands, the third mountain for visitors in Aspen to ski, is also a favorite of mine. It has more challenging terrain per square acre than the other mountains in Aspen. Aspen Highlands is often the mountain of choice by skiers with strong skills and strong physical endurance, but it is more than that, it is the advanced skier's sanctuary.

One of the special things about Aspen Highlands is that towards the top of the mountain, you can catch a free cat ride that will save you some steps on the hike up to some fantastic snow. It's possible to just take the cat ride and then pick a trail down from there, but it's even better to continue up on foot to conquer the trails that many people don't bother to invest sweat equity into. I advise that the cardio investment is worth the sweet return of soft snow, steep terrain, and a solitary vibe.

Lest you not put much value on that solitary vibe, let me describe it for you in more detail. Have you ever felt like the mountain is yours? Have you ever skied down for more than

20 minutes without seeing another person? It's the feeling of getting away, times 120. It's an awareness of the vastness and tranquility of nature. It's when we not only see nature, but we feel engulfed in it. Some feelings cannot adequately be described. The hike-to terrain at the top of Aspen Highlands is in that elite category of "beyond words" experiences. It's probably the closest thing to being an astronaut and landing on another planet as I will ever come.

If you dare, the cat at Aspen Highlands typically starts running in late December. To get there, take Exhibition lift to Loge Peak lift then follow the sign to the Highlands bowl. The cat operates only when snow and weather allow.

Buttermilk

The fourth mountain in Aspen is called Buttermilk. Beginner skiers and families with young children rave about this mountain. It has more beginner terrain than anywhere else in Colorado. Thirty-five percent of the terrain there provides beginner runs. As you progress, you may just want to stay at Buttermilk because thirty-nine percent of the terrain is intermediate. That's 74% of the mountain that's perfect for beginners and intermediates. No other mountain can boast numbers that high.

Buttermilk Mountain has been the location for the ESPN Winter X Games. Therefore, kids who have seen the ski and snowboard tricks in the air on TV can feel ultra cool trying their own tricks at Buttermilk. It's a comfortable, homey mountain that has been seen all over the world.

All four mountains in Aspen are worth checking out. This ski town with four mountains and seemingly limitless restaurants also has exceptional live music and nightlife.

When I first went on a quest to find my ski town home, a place where I could settle in and become a local, the availability and quality of live music was a key search criteria, right up there with the quality and quantity of moguls. Of all the ski towns that I spent lengthy stays in, Aspen had the best quality of live music. It's only a place like Aspen that can afford to have a venue like the Belly Up where countless music legends have played to small crowds through impeccable sound equipment. Aspen has at least ten music venues that cater to different types of musical genres. If the combination of skiing and live music or skiing and dancing are your perfect marriage, then Aspen is the place you will hear the sound of beauty.

By the way, if you like lazy rivers, the Aspen Recreation Center is the place to go. Only in Aspen is there a lazy river at the Rec center.

Both Vail and Aspen are Amazing and overwhelming, in a good way. So how can we move on from these famous mountains? The next chapter is for those of us who enjoy pleasant surprises.

7. Serendipitous Colorado Ski Resorts

Beaver Creek

I love Beaver Creek because I have experienced so many pleasant things that were not looked for. Whenever I am there, my expectations are constantly exceeded. It's the only place I feel that way about. Beaver Creek understands the impact of small gestures. Free, warm chocolate chip cookies every day at three o'clock are wonderful! Who would expect that from a mountain resort? And they have nice flair when they do it. A team of bakers in the tall, puffy, baker hats come out onto the snow in the base area with silver platters of warm chocolate chip cookies. It is possible to ski up to a baker, get a cookie and head right back to the lift. It's a warm reminder that the simple things in life, like kindness and generosity, bring smiles and warm one's heart.

There is a culture of kindness and generosity throughout the whole town. One restaurant gives free glasses of champagne at après and a hotel on the hill has free s'mores for its guests around the fire pits after the lifts close. For people who enjoy pleasant surprises, Beaver Creek is the place to go!

The resort also has an outdoor escalator to get to the lifts. A lot of resorts figure that we are physically fit so we can walk up stairs, but Beaver Creek understands that although we can walk up stairs, it's nice to take the escalator.

What is it about the customer service that is off the charts? It's the hourly worker who called the bus when I left my poles on it and after arranging for my poles to get back to me later, he went back into the office and brought out a safety patrol person who had some spare poles I could borrow in the meantime. It's the information desk worker who will talk with me and answer my questions for as long as I could think up questions to ask. It's the expedient workers in the ticket office. They intuitively understand when lingering enhances your experience and when lingering takes away from the experience.

The employees at Beaver Creek understand the concept of service and they go beyond it to provide service cheerfully. They outdo themselves by caring so well for their guests.

The Skiing is phenomenal. The mountain is paradise on earth, no matter what your skiing level is. Officially, the mountain is 19% beginner, 43% intermediate, 21% advanced (single diamond), 12% expert (double diamond), and 5% extreme terrain.

Unlike many mountains, I love that there are no undesirable trails that I have to take in order to get to where I want to go. The layout of the mountain is very good. Most of the slopes match the angle of the fall line. Many slopes provide excellent views. Multiple on-mountain lodges provide varied cuisine. The vibe at Beaver Creek is so positive. There is something to enjoy on every run.

The eating experience at Beaver Creek is exceptional. On Sundays, the largest mid-mountain lodge offered prime rib on its menu. It's great to walk into the lodge, immediately walk right up to the carving station, get prime rib, and after paying for the meal, be sitting down at a lovely table, eating within three minutes. Beaver Creek does a lot to keep lines short. More importantly, they offer food that is drastically more delicious than one would expect to be available mid-mountain.

Even at the large mid-mountain lodge, employees create opportunities for nice surprises. Many times after I paid for my meal, the cashier would reach into a large bucket of chocolate kisses and put a few on my tray. Sometimes a chocolate kiss is just the right ending to a meal. For people like me who like surprises, it was another serendipitous moment when once again small things in life brought a smile.

Have I said that I love moguls? The moguls at Beaver Creek are excellent. There are multiple runs where the moguls are laid out very well and it is easy to find a zipper line through them.

An unusual aspect of Beaver Creek is that it includes a collection of private clubs on the mountain. With three of the eight private clubs located in the Beaver Creek Ski Resort, private on-mountain dining and amenities are very convenient.

Another unusual and wonderful feature of the Beaver Creek Resort is that it has a ski-in, ski-out chapel right on the mountain. The chapel is shared by several different denominations and religions with back-to-back services for much of the day. So whether you are Jewish, Catholic or Protestant, you can easily take a run down to the church, leave your skis in the rack, and warm up while listening to an edifying message (without missing more than a few runs). It's very convenient and it's a blessing to the people who otherwise might not ski on Sunday.

The locals in Beaver Creek are very gracious. There is genuineness with their kindness. Unlike some resorts where neither seasonal visitors nor employees have a chance of friendship with any locals, the locals in Beaver Creek are welcoming and engaging. There is not only a civility, but also an openness and friendliness that make conversations delightful.

If you have a lot of money, then staying in Beaver Creek is optimal. If you love the mountain, but have less money, the town of Avon is a short shuttle bus ride away from the lifts and is much more affordable for many people. The shuttle bus system is very good and has many routes that frequent the larger hotels and developments. In addition, there is a section of Avon that has access to a gondola in town that goes directly to the mountain.

Beaver Creek is one of my favorite mountains because of the people, the terrain, the food, the customer service and the serendipity that only Beaver Creek provides.

Some resort somewhere used the tagline "Life as it should be." In my opinion, that's an accurate description of life in Beaver Creek.

By the way, Beaver Creek offers a lot more to do than skiing and eating. There is an ice skating rink that reminds me of the one at Rockefeller Center in New York City. There are certain events periodically on the ice so check into that when you go. There is also a tubing hill that is a lot of fun for adults and kids of all ages. Guided snowshoeing tours are also available.

For more sophisticated entertainment, there is the Vilar Performing Arts Center which provides symphonies, ballets, comedy, theater films and other artistic events.

Spas are also very popular in Beaver Creek. You will find them at the Hyatt, the Ritz, The Charter and other places. A massage or a facial is only a phone call away.

The "Not exactly roughing it" line associated with Beaver Creek is extremely modest. "The extreme opposite of roughing it" would be a more accurate description.

Breckenridge

Breckenridge is the whole package: fun slopes, great accommodations, fantastic town, cornices, moguls, shops, restaurants, and everything you might need.

Breckenridge is a great mountain and ski-in, ski-out condos are not difficult to find there. Breckenridge might be one of the best resorts for large groups on a modest budget.

The town of Breckenridge is quaint and offers shopping, restaurants, bars, and art galleries to fill your off mountain hours.

One unusual opportunity in Breckenridge is the opportunity to take a dog sled ride.

There is also a Nordic Center in-between the town and the ski slopes. It offers cross-country skiing and snowshoeing on trails in the White River National Forest.

For adventurous skiers, the Breckenridge ski resort has a bowl that usually has a cornice on it. With a little speed, you can fly off the edge, and drop down into the bowl.

Other good finds on Breckenridge are the wind drift areas. When it hasn't snowed in a few days, you can find soft snow that feels almost fresh in areas where the wind blown snow is collected by the uneven topography.

Even though Beaver Creek and Breckenridge are truly loveable, I would be missing out if I didn't experience other resorts. There is so much to tell. Each resort is unique, with its own strengths and weaknesses, and its own personality. Maybe resorts are somewhat like children to me, meaning I can love them all.

8. Colorado Mountains with Personality

Keystone

Keystone is a great family resort. Families with children love Keystone. Ice skaters enjoy the largest Zamboni-maintained outdoor skating rink in North America. It is five full acres large. Kids also like the tubing, ski-bikes, horse drawn sleigh rides, and snow forts.

With the resort being located 90 minutes from Denver, even families with children in the back seat find that the drive is manageable.

The hours of operation of the ski resort are unusually long. Keystone offers night skiing. Kids can ski anytime from 8:30 in the morning to 8:00 in the evening. Keystone has more night skiing terrain than any other ski resort in Colorado.

Some kids love the terrain park. It is over 60 acres large, has over 100 features and a park specific lift. It's an award winning terrain park, so for kids who are discerning when it comes to park features, Keystone's A51 Terrain Park is better than the best playground.

Locals and adventurers like the cat ride at Keystone. It accesses hundreds of skiable acres.

Personally, my favorite part of Keystone is a cozy coffee shop decorated with bookshelves and living room furniture. It's a great place to unwind whether you drink coffee or some other warm beverage.

For relaxing, the resort also has a 10,000 square foot spa. Every member of the family can find vacation relaxation.

Winter Park / Mary Jane

The terrain at Winter Park is enjoyable enough to warrant a trip from anywhere in the country. If you are an expert skier, you definitely want to get to Winter Park because 55% of the terrain is expert.

Winter Park has jumps throughout the mountain and huge jumps for the riders and skiers who like big air. The terrain is wonderfully fun. The Mary Jane side of the mountain is known for its moguls. Mogul lovers have many mogul runs, with moguls of all sizes, to enjoy. Have I said I love moguls? There is also a large glade area; it's more than just tree runs, it's skiing in the woods. If you are looking for a lot of skiable acres per dollar, then Winter Park's season pass is a great value.

If your music genre preferences include blues, it is likely that you will enjoy the nightlife in Winter Park. There are more live blues shows in the town of Winter Park than any other mountain I have seasoned at. There is also a great rib place in town, delicious restaurants if you like steak, and surprisingly good sweet potato fries on the mountain.

Arapahoe Basin

Locals and lovers of steep terrain call Arapahoe Basin "A-Basin." It may be a small resort with less than 1,000 skiable acres, but it attracts hardcore skiers from all around Colorado. It has 10% beginner and 30% intermediate trails. However, its reputation is based on its 37% advanced and 23% expert runs. The mountain offers more challenge per acre than most.

The mountain vibe is hardcore. The summit elevation is 13,050 feet and the base elevation is 10,780 feet, which makes the vertical drop 2,270 feet. The East Wall, known for its hiking terrain and powder runs, makes A-Basin the highest skiable terrain in North America.

There is a feeling of outdoor expedition in the air, perhaps because half of the mountain is above timberline or perhaps because one of the mountain's signature runs is one of Colorado's longest and steepest trails. If you like long and steep, be sure not to miss "Pallavicini." Ski it until your heart is content, or 1.5 miles, whichever comes first. Locals who love to ski love that this mountain offers bowl skiing all the way into early summer. It's so hard for some people to declare the ski season over and because of A-Basin, they don't have to do that until summer time.

The amenities at A-Basin may be commensurate with the size of the resort, however the camaraderie among the skiers is off the charts. Tailgating parties in the parking lot are common. There are even select parking spots that come with their own picnic tables that can be reserved for a small fee. The prime tailgating area is called the Beach and spans from the parking area near the Pallavicini lift to the Mountain Express lift.

Special events like scavenger hunts and other community events on the mountain happen every year. For the physically fit, there is a grueling 10-hour competition to see how many runs off the Pallavicini lift a team of two can ski in one day. It's called the Enduro. Endure it if you can; it may take over 100 miles of skiing to win that competition.

By the way, the nickname for the Pallavicini lift is "Pali", which most people pronounce as "Polly." People who spend most of their day skiing Pali are often known as "pali-heads." The bottom trail that takes you out of the Pallavicini run is referred to as the "Poly-wog."

A-Basin is a resort not to be missed. Skimag.com included it in its list of Top 10 resorts for Character (2013). Forbes included it in its Top 10 ski resorts in the U.S., ranked by "awesomeness." SKI Magazine included the Basin in its list of 10 best mountains you've never skied. You are missing out if you don't try it.

Arapahoe Basin and Loveland are two of the country's highest-elevation ski areas so they usually start blowing snow earlier than most other mountains. A-Basin often earns the award for "First Resort to Open".

Loveland Ski Resort

The first time I skied at Loveland, I skied there on my way to the airport. If you are headed to the airport from Vail, Breckenridge or Winter Park and are tight for ski hours before you leave, then you will really appreciate Loveland giving you the opportunity to get some runs in. It is also a fun mountain for local kids.

Loveland's statistics make it sound as if it might be similar to A-Basin. Its summit elevation is 13,010 and the base elevation is 10,800 feet, so the vertical drop is 2,200 feet, which is only 70 feet less than A-Basin. However, the vibe is like night and day. At Loveland, families and kids are everywhere.

Loveland has more skiable acres (1,800 acres) than A-Basin (1,000 acres), so there is plenty of room for children to have more than enough space as they go down the slopes.

The longest run on the mountain is two miles, which is among the longest in Colorado. So if you like your runs long, head to Loveland and you won't be disappointed.

Copper Mountain

Since I just finished thinking about all the families at Loveland, Copper Mountain came to mind. I was skiing at Copper and had gone into the lodge for lunch when I saw someone who looked a lot like my brother from Atlanta. I figured it was just someone who looked like him, but I walked across the lunchroom to find out. To my surprise, it was my brother. He was as surprised as I was. There are all kinds of things that can make a ski day great. Sometimes it's running into someone that you really want to ski with. I hadn't skied with my brother in more than ten years. He was a racer in high school and college and had been offered a scholarship to the University of Colorado. I was a mogul lover; have I mentioned that? However, in our youth, we had skied quite a bit together. His birthday is at the end of December and some years we would head to Killington, Vermont to celebrate on the slopes. The runs we did together at Copper were reminiscent of those days when we both developed a love for the childhood delight of speed and agility that the snow provided. I have very fond memories of Copper, but I don't remember much about the mountain. Like all the best vacations, it's the people that matter most.

The U.S. Ski Team trains at Copper. If it's good enough for the U.S. Ski Team and my brother, you'll probably find it is good for you too.

For those of you who are technologically inclined, Copper Mountain has Sherpa, the on-the-mountain audio intelligence app. Sherpa was introduced by Copper Mountain Resort for the 2013-14 ski season and is described as a "virtual mountain guide." If you are wondering how that works… When you get near something worth knowing about, Sherpa will let you know.

Copper's Sherpa App was voted the 2013/2014 Best Use of Mobile Technology by the National Ski Areas Association. Sherpa provides hands-free, real-time insider intelligence, across the entire mountain.

In Spring 2015, Copper handed over the controls of Sherpa to everyone, allowing for an open-sourced mountain. Guests can share their comments and tips about this mountain on the app.

Exploring More Resorts

If there was a map with all the ski resorts in the Rocky Mountains, then that map would be huge and it could even lead you back in time. Well perhaps not actually back in time, but if you want to feel like you went back to a previous era where bandits and cowboys tell their stories, then there are mountains for you.

9. Mountains With Historical Feel

There are some resorts that can provide moments of feeling like you have stepped back in time. Telluride and Steamboat have historic vibes and are vividly different from other ski resorts. Leaving the ordinariness of everyday life for one of these resorts, although not time travel, can leave a person wide-eyed.

Telluride

Telluride is considered by many people to have the best views. Even the unobservant who go to Telluride find themselves standing on top of the mountain and looking around. It's a place where you might sigh a breath of wonder and appreciation that land can be this beautiful.

The first time I went to Telluride, I was on a ski vacation with several friends. At that time, I had skied hundreds of ski days and was a strong intermediate or a weak expert skier. The thing I remember most was that Telluride was the first place where I was scared. Lest you be concerned, I was scared in a wonderful way. It was the kind of scared that you might feel as the rollercoaster changes from its ascent to its descent. It's the kind of scared that makes you scream with adrenaline while still holding a smile on your face. Telluride feels steep. When you look down the slope and the town at the bottom looks smaller than your dad's train set, you feel the extremeness of the vertical feet you are about to descend.

Another of my favorite things about Telluride is its skinny chutes. To this day, my favorite chute in the entire world is in Telluride. Whenever I arrive at the narrow entrance and look down at the sharp angle of the slope falling beneath me, it puts a smile on my face and adrenaline in my blood stream.

Steeps, powder, and tree skiing are the types of runs most of us associate with Telluride, so it is hard to reconcile that somehow 60% of the mountain is beginner or intermediate terrain. Lovers of this mountain tend to be in the steeps, so the large beginner area is almost always uncrowded.

Even more surprising is that almost all levels of skiers can experience the stunning views of Telluride. Just go to the top of Gold Hill Express (Lift 14) and take in the incredible views. From the top of Lift 14, beginner skiers can ski the "See Forever" trail to the base of the mountain. People who do this groomed run rave about the scenic vistas.

Not only is the mountain beautiful in Telluride, the town is also incredibly charming. Parts of it look perfect enough for a movie scene. There are beautiful Victorian homes lining the streets in town.

The town was founded in 1878. It was originally named Columbia, but the townspeople changed the name to Telluride in 1887. Back then it was a budding mining town. There are various versions of the story on how the town got its name, but it seems that Telluride was named after tellurium, a nonmetallic element associated with rich mineral deposits of gold and silver. Nearly five thousand people lived in Telluride at the height of the gold rush. At the turn of the century, more millionaires (per capita) lived in Telluride than in New York City. The mine, called the Tomboy Mine, provided more than $360 million dollars worth of gold.

Butch Cassidy began robbing banks in Telluride. His first heist was at the San Miguel Valley Bank, which was at the corner of Pine Street and Main Street. As the story goes, once out of town, the three outlaws raced their horses as fast as they could go. Unfortunately for Butch, they crossed paths with Harry Adsit. Butch Cassidy and one of his partners in crime had both previously worked for Mr. Adsit on his ranch. The outlaws had no doubt he could identify them to the authorities. This became the point of no return for the bank robbers. Harry Adsit did inform the pursuing posse who the bank robbers were and the direction they were heading. From then on, the law would follow them for thousands of miles and for years.

The loot from that robbery in Telluride, which changed their lives forever and put them on the run, was almost $25,000. It was never recovered.

If you go to Telluride, you can see the plaque on the side of the Mahr building, which was the original site of the San Miguel Valley Bank.

Telluride's boom days busted and many of the town's mines shut down by the early 1950s. Families left town and Telluride temporarily became a ghost town.

In 1972, a wealthy entrepreneur from Beverly Hills envisioned building a ski resort. It opened with five lifts and a day lodge. Six years later, he sold it to two Colorado natives who purchased the ski area and transformed Telluride into a world-class resort. In 1985, they built Mountain Village. While the base of Telluride is at 8750 feet, and the summit is 13,320 feet, Mountain Village is located at 9,500 feet. Mountain Village has modern alpine elegance that compliments the rustic charm of Telluride.

In 2004, the resort was purchased by Chuck Horning and his partners and has expanded into Black Iron Bowl, Palmyra Peak, the Gold Hill Chutes and Revelation Bowl.

Nowadays, over two thousand people live in the town of Telluride and over one thousand people live year round in

Mountain Village. Plus, thousands of people visit the area every year.

A pedestrian gondola connects the town of Telluride and the town of Mountain Village. It is free and it runs from 7 AM to midnight. Most resorts only use their gondolas for skiing, so it is special to take the gondola into town for dinner and when returning see another beautiful view, this time viewing the lights in the distance.

Telluride's gondola is the first and only free public transportation of its kind in the United States. The trip between the town of Telluride and Mountain Village would be eight miles long by car. However, by gondola, it is only three miles away. A car rental is not necessary in Telluride.

Approximately 2.25 million passengers ride the gondola annually. Over 30 million riders have been transported since the gondola officially opened in 1996. If you bring a pet with you, there is no problem; approximately 25 percent of the cabins are pet accessible.

Most lodging is ski-in/ski-out or just a short walk to the slopes. The restaurants and shops are also conveniently located within walking distance. There is no shortage of places to eat or drink since there are over 60 restaurants, coffee shops and bars.

One thing you may notice is that the locals in Telluride do not seem to be fans of chain stores nor chain restaurants. Last time I was there, there was not a single business that was part of a large chain. Although there may be a restaurant owner who owns two restaurants, for the most part the locals regulate the businesses that are allowed into town. When you are in the middle of a Big Mac attack, you may be longing for a chain. However, all the mom and pop places give the town a quaint feel. This vacation spot is worlds away from ordinary, everyday life.

The town looks a lot like a movie set for an old western film. The buildings are reminiscent of the mining town that it once was. When you go to Telluride, you may find yourself wanting to take photos, even if that is not your modus operandi (M.O.).

There are movie stars and artists who own homes in Telluride. Which came first, the stars and artists or the festivals, is a discussion that may end up a lot like the chicken or the egg. The Mountainfilm Festival, Telluride Film Festival, Bluegrass Festival and Jazz Festival are known for attracting the best filmmakers and musicians in the world.

Telluride has many events including musical, cultural, culinary, scientific, athletic and unusual. By unusual, I mean very unusual. Telluride has a Mushroom Festival that celebrates the many uses of fungi. I'm not sure if there is another place in the United States that celebrates fungi. Many locals like the Blue and Brews event. It is held in September and signifies the start of fall colors and the coming of ski season.

Telluride typically enjoys an average snowfall of 309 inches per year and although it was not my experience the year I was there, many people have told me Telluride usually has over 300 days of sunshine each year. My experience was it snowed so often that the snow conditions were bliss.

The winter when I was there, I was more likely to fly out of Montrose airport than Telluride airport. I did that because I was often able to get a direct flight from Montrose. The airport is only a one hour and fifteen minute drive from Telluride on well-maintained state highways through the San Juan Mountains. However, I did use Telluride Regional Airport (TEX) a couple of times. The regional airport is located on Last Dollar Road in Telluride. At 9,070 feet above sea level, the airport offers picturesque views of the San Juan Mountains. TEX is seven miles, or a 10-minute drive from the

Telluride Resort and Mountain Village. Shuttle services and car rentals are available, and many Telluride and Mountain Village hotels offer complimentary pickup and drop-off services. Mountain Aviation, a private jet charter, flies into Telluride Regional Airport, as does Peak Aero Group and other private jets. This is an added luxury to traveling to Telluride.

From reading this section, you can see why people love Telluride. The views, terrain, history, and town are like medicine for the soul.

Other Resorts in Southwest Colorado

Telluride may be the most acclaimed ski resort in Southwest Colorado, but there are other smaller ski resorts worth skiing: Crested Butte, Purgatory at Durango Mountain Resort, Silverton, and Wolf Creek. Like Telluride, they offer breathtaking scenery and authentic mountain town experiences.

Crested Butte

Crested Butte's small historic town is welcoming. This place is reminiscent of a simpler life and time. Not only are there no chain stores here, there is not even a stoplight. At this resort, you really feel like you are getting away from your normal life. It is an unspoiled setting and it inspires adventure.

Purgatory

Although its name might lead you to believe otherwise, Purgatory is a family destination resort with spectacular scenery. Purgatory Mountain was named in 1776 when explorers lost some of their party and the bodies were never found. Purgatory Ski Area opened in 1965. Purgatory was later renamed Durango Mountain resort. However, in 2015, James Coleman purchased the resort and changed the name of the 50 year old ski area back to Purgatory. Near the Purgatory Ski Area, the historic railroad town of Durango has a 12,000 square foot museum with railroad cars, mint condition engines, and bountiful railroad memorabilia.

Silverton Mountain

I've heard people talk about Silverton Mountain at several of the mountains I've been at. Skiing enthusiasts are passionate about Silverton. At first I wasn't interested when I heard that there was only one lift, but then it was explained to me that Silverton offers chairlift-served guided skiing. Moreover, the terrain is only advanced and expert. I loved it when I heard that at Silverton, the average total snowfall of over 400 inches exceeds the amount of daily visitors. This mountain needs to be experienced to be understood. To experience this mountain is to appreciate it.

Wolf Creek

Wolf Creek is one of the oldest ski resorts still operating in Colorado. They opened in 1939 and today there are some heart warming old time values at this family owned and operated resort. Wolf Creek has more natural snowfall than any other ski resort in Colorado. It receives about 430 inches of snow each year.

Steamboat

The other Colorado ski resort very worth discussing is Steamboat. It is located in the northern part of Colorado. It is the only ski resort in Colorado that is known for its champagne powder. Steamboat has 3,000 skiable acres and 3,668 vertical feet. It's no wonder that Steamboat has produced 88 Winter Olympians, more Olympians than any other resort town in North America. I'm told that in Steamboat, kids learn to ski as soon as they can walk.

When I took a five-week ski vacation, I skied every day except for one and that day I went to one of Steamboat's acclaimed hot springs. Steamboat is known for its hot springs, and I was not disappointed. However, the thing I remember the best about Steamboat was how I loved a mogul run that was directly under a chairlift. Like I said, I love moguls. I did laps on that one run for many days. I wasn't the only one; it seemed like all the mogul lovers were there. Some of the bumpers were extremely impressive, others were not, but there was an unusual sense of camaraderie among the skiers. We had gravitated to that slope out of a shared love for challenge and shared enjoyment of agility. I made many friends on that run because after a few runs it would become apparent that I was going about the same speed as someone else and so when we got to the bottom whichever person was slightly ahead would hesitate so that we could take the chairlift together and get acquainted. It is especially fun to ski moguls with a buddy. Two friends side by side or four friends following behind each other, the most fun is had when it is directly down a big mogul field.

The vibe on the hill may have a strong sense of community, but the vibe in town has a strong sense of cowboy. I'm surprised there aren't more country music concerts in that town. Going out in Steamboat is fun and there are many places to make memories.

10. Colorado Ski Resort Numbers

The ski towns in Colorado are amazing. Anyone can find the size resort and the terrain difficulty that they prefer. The resorts vary in steepness and snowfall. The resorts also differ in vibe and amenities.

For those of you who like to look at the statistics, they are on the next page. You can see that if you are looking for most skiable acres in Colorado, then Vail is top, Snowmass is second, and Winter Park is third in skiable acres. If you are looking for most beginner terrain, Buttermilk can become your mountain.

The statistics can help you find what you are looking for. If you are looking for most expert terrain, you might want to make your travel arrangements to Winter Park, Vail or Steamboat.

If you recently became an intermediate, you will enjoy Snowmass and Aspen, and you can ski both of them in the same ski trip. Loveland and Sunlight also offer great terrain for new intermediates.

Advanced intermediates may choose Arapahoe Basin and Copper. There is also a high percentage of advanced terrain at Howelsen, so if a smaller mountain suits you, and you are an advanced skier or rider, you might like it there.

For experts, Telluride has the largest vertical drop of 4,425 feet and Snowmass has the second largest with 4,406 feet. The highest peaks are at Silverton and Telluride.

COLORADO RESORTS	LIFTS	TRAILS	SKIABLE ACRES	% TERRAIN BY DIFFICULTY BEG/INT/ADV/EX
VAIL	31	193	5,289	18/29/53
SNOWMASS	20	94	3,332	6/47/17/30
KEYSTONE	20	131	3148	14/29/57
WINTER PARK	26	143	3,081	8/18/19/55
STEAMBOAT	16	165	2,965	14/42/44
BRECKENRIDGE	34	187	2908	14/31/19/36
COPPER	22	140	2,465	21/25/36/18
TELLURIDE	18	127	2,000	23/36/41
BEAVER CREEK	24	150	1832	19/43/38
SILVERTON	1	69	1,819	0/0/100
LOVELAND	10	93	1,800	13/41/22/24
POWDERHORN	5	63	1,600	20/50/30
WOLF CREEK	7	77	1,600	20/35/25/20
CRESTED BUTTE	15	121	1,547	21/57/16
PURGATORY	10	88	1,360	20/45/35
ASPEN HIGHLANDS	5	119	1,028	18/30/16/36
ARAPAHOE BASIN	8	109	960	10/30/37/23
MONARCH	8	63	800	14/28/58
ELDORA	11	53	680	20/50/15/15
ASPEN	8	76	673	0/48/26/26
BUTTERMILK	9	44	470	35/39/21/5
SUNLIGHT	3	67	470	20/55/20/5
GRANBY RANCH	6	41	406	30/50/20
SKI COOPER	4	26	400	30/40/30
HOWELSEN	4	17	50	25/20/55/0

All this being said, the statistics don't tell the whole story. On my list of places I'd really like to get to someday is Powderhorn. It is the largest flat-topped mountain in the world. I hear the tree skiing, powder and uncrowded slopes may make this resort worth the trip.

There are some great low cost ski resorts in Colorado including Howelsen, Ski Cooper, Ski Grandby Ranch, Monarch, and Sunlight. If you are looking for a great price, you might like one of those mountains.

If you are in Boulder or Denver, you may want to head to Eldora Ski Resort. It is only 21 miles from Boulder and 45 miles from Denver. Eldora has 500 snowmaking acres which is more than any other resort in Colorado.

Wolf Creek, with 430 inches annually, wins Colorado's snow contest. Loveland's 422 average annual inches of snow is not far behind. Personally, I need to get myself to Silverton for some of that 400 inches per year. However, no one is complaining at Monarch or A-Basin; they are enjoying 350 inches of fresh snow every year. You can look at the snowfall for all of the resorts in Colorado on the next page.

COLORADO RESORTS	PEAK	BASE	VERTICAL DROP	AVERAGE ANNUAL SNOWFALL IN INCHES
WOLF CREEK	11,904'	10300'	1,604'	430
LOVELAND	13,010'	10800'	2,210'	422
SILVERTON	13,487'	10400'	3,287'	400
VAIL	11,570'	8120'	3450'	354
ARAPAHOE BASIN	13,050'	10,780'	2,270'	350
MONARCH	11,952'	10790'	1,162'	350
STEAMBOAT	10,568'	6900'	3,668'	347
WINTER PARK	12,060'	9000'	3,060'	327
BEAVER CREEK	11,440'	8,100'	3,339'	310
TELLURIDE	13,150'	8750'	4,425'	309
ASPEN HIGHLANDS	12,392'	8040'	3,635'	300
ASPEN MOUNTAIN	11,212'	7945'	3,267'	300
ELDORA	10,800'	9200'	1,600'	300
SNOWMASS	12,510'	8104'	4,406'	300
CRESTED BUTTE	12,162'	9375'	3,062'	289
COPPER	12,313'	9703'	2,601'	269
PURGATORY	10,822'	8739'	2,029'	260
POWDERHORN	9,850'	8200'	1,650'	250
SKI COOPER	11,700'	10500'	1,200'	250
SUNLIGHT	9,895'	7885'	2,010'	250
KEYSTONE	12,408'	9,280'	3128'	235
GRANBY RANCH	9,202'	8202'	1,000'	220
BUTTERMILK	9,900'	7870'	2,030'	200
HOWELSEN	7,136'	6696'	440'	150
BRECKENRIDGE	12,998'	9,600'	3,398'	108

There is nothing like a Colorado ski town. Approximately 20% of all U.S. visits are to Colorado.

Colorado ski resorts give visitors the whole package: fun towns, cool vibes, great mountains, fast chairs, and the most spectacular scenery a skier could hope for. However, if you have never been to Idaho and you find it hard to believe that you are missing out on something by your lack of travel to this state, you are the person I wrote the next chapter for. You may be surprised.

11. Constant Pitch Steeps in Idaho

Idaho is a place where the only thing better than the spectacular scenery is the constant pitch of the steeps. There are 18 ski resorts, 95 chair lifts, 794 runs, over 18,500 skiable acres and nearly 28,000 vertical feet of exhilarating terrain. In Idaho, the slopes have champagne powder.

Sun Valley

If you have only been to one ski mountain in Idaho, it was probably Sun Valley. Sun Valley is a resort city in central Idaho. Among skiers, the words "Sun Valley" refer to the alpine ski areas on Bald Mountain and Dollar Mountain. Bald Mountain is the main ski mountain adjacent to Ketchum. Dollar Mountain is the easier mountain for novice and lower intermediate skiers.

Sun Valley is a true anomaly among modern ski resortsm which is likely the result of having once been the most accessible ski town in the country, then later becoming one of the least accessible. As the story is told, in 1935 Count Felix Schaffgotsch was commissioned by Union Pacific Railroad to begin a search for the perfect North American ski destination. After months of exploring the western United States, he found Ketchum Valley and was smitten by the area's terrain features. Averell Harriman, chairman of Union Pacific Railroad agreed and after just seven months of construction, Sun Valley opened for business in the winter of 1936.

The railroad loved Sun Valley not only for its beauty and climate, but also for its proximity to Ketchum, a stop on its railway line. At a time when commercial air travel had yet to take off, the railroad put the resort on the map by offering a straight shot from Hollywood.

The resort was meant to be America's first destination ski resort, an answer to popular European resorts like St. Moritz. Sun Valley has been a seasonal home to the rich and famous since first being brought to public attention by Ernest Hemingway in the late 1930s. Life magazine also gave the resort a "shout out" when it featured a skier riding Sun Valley's new chairlift on a 1937 Life magazine cover. There are still remnants of its heritage as a getaway for the rich and famous; Bruce Willis, Arnold Schwarzenegger, and Tom Hanks own homes there.

Even though Sun Valley is a little tricky to get to today (it is a three-hour drive from Boise), it is worth the visit. The area is beautifully trapped in time. There are vast areas that are free of development. The location is surrounded by three different mountain ranges, including the largest roadless area in the lower 48 states.

I liked the way Langely McNeal, a nationally ranked ski-cross racer described Sun Valley. He said, "Sun Valley feels like a ski town built around skiing, not a real estate development with a ski resort built on to add value."

If you go to Sun Valley, be sure to hit Warm Springs ski run on Bald Mountain. Zach Crist, X Games gold medalist and lifetime Sun Valley local has skied it. Zach says, "Warm Springs has this cult-like following... some skiers are so addicted to the speed and thrill, they ski it every day all winter long." It is considered by many to be the best stretch of downhill in the country.

The run has been described as a two mile long, top to bottom screamer that charges straight through a natural gully with banked sidewalls before opening up to the width of a California freeway. It never wavers from the fall line and maintains an average pitch of 35 degrees without a single blind turn to slow you down.

Sun Valley is a ski destination that every skier, and especially every snowboarder who enjoys cruising at high speed, should have on their bucket list. What makes Sun Valley special? It has an abundance of constant pitch terrain at varying degrees of difficulty. No flats, no plateaus; the terrain all pitches downhill. It is also notable for its substantial vertical drop. Lovers of this mountain are often lovers of speed. The constant pitch makes it easy to see far downhill, which makes it safe to pick up speed.

Also noticeable are the empty chairs on the chairlifts. Sun Valley's lift capacity is almost 30,000 skiers/riders per hour, yet there are only 3,000 people on the slopes on an average day. It's unlikely that you will encounter long lines.

Sun Valley may have been aptly named because the sun shines 80 percent of the ski season, but I don't go there for the sun. What makes Sun Valley an important ski resort to visit is the constant pitch, absence of wind, and ample lift capacity.

Just so you know, Sun Valley is a very family-friendly destination. You will see a lot of families there. There is a wide range of activities for the kids.

There are also a lot of adaptive sports programs for the disabled. The Sun Valley region boasts a wide variety of year round adaptive sports programs including the local Disabled Sports USA Chapter; Sun Valley Adaptive Sports, Wood River Ability Program, Sage Brush Equine Training Center for the Handicapped, and Camp Rainbow Gold, a program for youth with cancer.

Olympic medalists from Sun Valley include Gretchen Fraser, Christin Cooper, Picabo Street, snowboarder Kaitlyn Farrington, and disabled skier Muffy Davis, a founding and honorary board member of Sun Valley Adaptive Sports. All five have runs named after them on Bald Mountain.

In case you were curious, Warren Miller, the famous ski film producer, wintered in Sun Valley from 1946-1949. He was in his early 20s back then. As the story goes, people say he first lived in a car and small trailer in the River Run parking lot and later rented an unheated garage for five dollars per month. He sublet floor space in the garage to friends to sleep in sleeping bags for fifty cents per night. One of those friends was Edward Scott, the future inventor of the lightweight aluminum ski pole. While in Sun Valley, Warren Miller transformed from ski bum to ski instructor to ski filmmaker. Warren Miller's ski films are iconic. He has produced over 750 sports films. His skiing films are known for their photography, narrative humor, and broad appeal.

Just so you know how to plan, Sun Valley is scheduled to host the U.S. Alpine Championships 2018. They last hosted the event in 2016. Before that, they hadn't hosted the Championships since 1951.

In addition to Sun Valley, there are ski resorts all over Idaho.

Schweitzer Mountain Resort

Schweitzer Mountain Resort has the most skiable acres in all of Idaho. With 2900 acres of skiable snow, Schweitzer provides all the turns you could hope for. When you take a break, I recommend that you stand at the top of the mountain so that you can see three mountain ranges, Canada and three states. That's a lot to see in one ski break! By the way, Schweitzer has a sister resort in Canada called Whitewater Ski Resort. It is just a short drive from Nelson, British Columbia, which was voted North America's best ski town. The resort promotes its "family-friendly groomers, gentle glades, extreme steeps and deeps, and endless backcountry." Whitewater is known for its authentic ski/snowboard setting.

When you stop looking at the view from the top and get back to skiing, you will find that since the place is so big, the terrain offers a lot of variety (smooth corduroy groomers to wide open bowls and tree runs).

Whether you are going down or going up, speed is not an issue at Schweitzer, where you will appreciate "Stella", Idaho's only six person, high speed lift.

Schweitzer has 92 trails plus open bowl skiing. Its terrain is 10% Beginner, 40% Intermediate, 35% Advanced, and 15% Expert. If you like groomed runs, the longest groomed run at Schweitzer, "Little Blue Ridge Run", is two miles long.

Schweitzer offers twilight skiing from 3 PM to 7 PM. Other things that can be done in the evening are: Hermit's Hollow Tubing Center, dining at Chimney Rock, beer & wine tasting, and shopping in the village.

If you are looking for something different, Schweitzer offers snowbiking, one of the fastest growing winter sports. If you are picturing those bikes that have sleds under the wheel area, at Schweitzer it's different. It's fat tire snowbiking on Nordic trails. They have over 32 kilometers of relatively flat trails. It's a great way to spend an hour or a day. You can also use those trails for Nordic skiing or snowshoeing.

For my friends with young children, I'll mention that Schweitzer offers professional daycare for infants and young children who are not skiers, so that you can go and enjoy the slopes.

Bogus Basin

Bogus Basin Recreational Association is a 501(c)(3) charitable organization. It operates under an all volunteer board of directors. A professional staff manages all day-to-day operations and Bogus employs over 600 seasonal employees each winter. Bogus Basin is only 16.5 miles from Boise. Bogus Basin provides affordable skiing on 2600 acres for every ability and interest.

Brundage Mountain

Brundage Mountain is known for its powder-packed glades and luxuriously wide groomed runs. It's a solid mountain with 1,500 inbounds skiable acres, 1,800 feet of vertical drop, 5 lifts, and 320 inches of annual snowfall. Even though 1,500 acres is accessible inbounds, there are 17,000 backcountry acres accessible via snowcat.

Brundage is a great snowcat skiing and riding destination because of the huge number of snowcat accessible acres. There are benefits to using snowcats. For example, snowcat skiing is usually less expensive than heli-skiing. It is also a lot easier than hiking, so it enables people who only exercise on weekends to get to the deep powder, without tiring themselves out on the way.

Grand Targhee

Grand Targhee gets more than 500 inches of snow per year. Grand Targhee is located in the Caribou-Targhee National Forest where the snow is light powder. There are five lifts on 2600 acres and the lack of lift lines creates an uncrowded, wide-open, spacious skiing experience. The vertical drop is 2270 feet. Inbounds, the mountain is ideal for intermediates, since 70 percent of its runs are intermediate.

One of the hallmarks of the Grand Targhee Resort experience is a Snowcat Adventure on Peaked Mountain. Just twelve skiers on a huge powder reserve of over 600 acres and up to 20,000 vertical feet enables private skiing experiences.

The resort also has a tubing park and 15km of Nordic trails. Guided backcountry skiing and snowshoeing are also enjoyed at Grand Targhee.

Even though most people know about Sun Valley, it is notable that three resorts have more skiable acres: Schweitzer, Bogus Basin and Grand Targhee.

IDAHO RESORTS	LIFTS	TRAILS	SKIABLE ACRES
Schweitzer	9	92	2900
Bogus Basin	9	53	2600
Grand Targhee	5	72	2402
Sun Valley Resort	19	80	2054
Lost Trail	8	50	1800
Silver Mountain	7	74	1600
Brundage Mountain	5	46	1500
Soldier Mountain	3	36	1150
Pebble Creek Ski Area	3	54	1100
Tamarack Resort	6	32	900
Kelly Canyon	5	26	640
Lookout Pass	4	34	540
Cottonwood Butte	2	7	260
Pomerelle	3	24	250
Bald Mountain Ski Area	2	19	140
Little Ski Hill	1	5	50
Snowhaven	2	7	40
Magic Mountain	3	20	20

Idaho ski resorts that are medium sized:

▪ Lost Trail is a family owned resort on the Continental Divide where Montana and Idaho meet. Locals consider it a hidden gem. Here is a good tip when you go to this mountain, keep track of the weather. The benefit of Lost Trail being closed two or three days a week is that the powder accumulates, therefore you can ski deep, untouched powder days after it stops snowing.

- Silver Mountain is different from most other ski resorts because you ride the gondola from the base village up to the slopes and then at the end of the day take the three-mile gondola ride back down to the village. There are no mountain roads or hairpin turns to deal with when you go to this resort. In addition to snow skiing, Idaho's largest indoor waterpark is at the Morning Star Lodge. There are indoor surf lessons available at Silver Rapids Indoor Waterpark Resort.

- Pebble Creek has 54 runs on 1,100 skiable acres. The terrain is 12% beginner, 35% intermediate and 53% advanced. The area is serviced by three triple chairlifts. There are two groomed terrain parks with a continually changing and growing array of boxes and features.

- Soldier Mountain is a three-lift, 867 vertical foot resort with 1,150 skiable acres. It used to be owned by Hollywood actor Bruce Willis, but it was transitioned to a nonprofit group in 2013.

Idaho has a lot of small resorts:

- Bald Mountain has 140 acres, one rope tow and one T bar. It's "the best little ski hill in Idaho."

- Kelly Canyon, a smaller resort, offers 1,000 feet of vertical on 640 acres for a $40 lift ticket.

- Little Ski Hill is a small alpine hill served by a T-bar providing 405 vertical feet of terrain.

- Lookout Pass is on the Idaho/Montana border.

- Magic Mountain has 11 trails on 120 acres and 740 feet of vertical.

- Pomerelle has 250 acres and caters specifically to families enjoying and learning to ski or board.

- Snowhaven is the smallest of the bunch with 40 acres. It is the place of many childhood memories for local residents.
- Tamarack is a family friendly resort that has 900 skiable acres for vacationers, groups, and weddings.
- CottonWood Butte has 260 skiable acres. Last time I checked, the resort's home page played on its location, "Located just beyond the North Idaho Correctional Institute, so take a little drive and escape to the Cottonwood Butte!"

IDAHO RESORTS	PEAK	BASE	VERTICAL DROP
Sun Valley Resort	9150	5150	3400
Tamarack Resort	7700	4900	2800
Schweitzer Mountain Resort	6400	4000	2400
Grand Targhee	9862	8000	2270
Silver Mountain Resort	6300	4100	2200
Pebble Creek Ski Area	8560	6300	2200
Lost Trail Powder Mountain	8200	6400	1800
Brundage Mountain Resort	7640	5840	1800
Bogus Basin	7582	5800	1800
Soldier Mountain Resort	7177	5752	1425
Lookout Pass	5650	4500	1150
Pomerelle Mountain Resort	9000	8000	1000
Kelly Canyon	6600	5600	1000
Cottonwood Butte	5125	4280	845
Magic Mountain Resort	7240	6500	740
Bald Mountain Ski Area	4800	4000	684
Payette Lakes - Little Ski Hill	5405	5000	405
Snowhaven	5600	5200	400

When it comes to vertical drop in Idaho, Sun Valley tops the chart. I'm thinking about steeps and I'm craving some vertical drop right now. You don't want to drop out of this book now though because the next chapter provides the most important information. It is all about which mountain is the best of the best.

12. The Best Resorts in the Rockies

The Rocky Mountains, commonly known as the Rockies, pass through the states of New Mexico, Colorado, Utah, Wyoming, Montana, and Idaho, and extend into Alaska and Canada. You have now read about all of the ski resorts in the Rocky Mountain Range in the continental United States.

The Rocky Mountain Range actually represents a series of many separate mountain ranges, rather than one uninterrupted mountain chain. The width of the Rocky Mountain system varies between 70 and 300 miles. The Rocky Mountains extend 3,000 miles from central New Mexico to Northwest Alaska. Mt. Elbert in Colorado is the highest peak at 14,431 feet above sea level.

In the future, I might write about ski resorts in Alaska and Canada, or in California, Washington and Oregon. However, I decided to write about the continental U.S. Rocky Mountain ski resorts first because many of my first loves are here: that mogul run under the lift in Steamboat, that chute in Telluride, that bowl in Vail, that cozy condo in Breckenridge, that art gallery in Breckenridge, those cookies in Beaver Creek, and that customer service in Beaver Creek.

One never knows how their life will change drastically in an instant. Looking back, the decision to get affordable skiing and lodging at Winter Park/Mary Jane for a season changed my life for the better. I ended up going there three seasons in a row. Winter Park/Mary Jane deepened my love for the sport I was already passionate about. I got that lodging rental through a friend of a friend of a friend. It started me on a lifestyle of seasonal rentals and monthly rentals at multiple resorts.

So it is finally time to rank what I think is the best of the best of these Rocky Mountain resorts that I've told you about. The rankings all depend on what a person is looking for.

Best powder:
1. Alta
2. Snow Bird
3. Solitude
4. Steamboat

Best bowls:
1. Vail
2. Breckenridge

Best steeps:
1. Telluride has a lot of great steeps.
2. Jackson Hole has Alta Zero and Corbet's Couloir

Best moguls:
1. Mary Jane
2. Vail
3. Beavercreek
4. Deer Valley
5. Steamboat

Top resort if you like views:
1. Telluride

Top resorts if you want to see amazing tricks and jumps when you are in or near the park:
1. Winter Park

Top resort if you like your snow groomed:
1. Deer Valley

Other top resorts if you like your snow groomed:
2. Beaver Creek
3. Keystone
4. Aspen
5. Turner (where more than half of the 3,000 acres are groomed).

Top Resorts if you like to ski fast:
1. Sun Valley
2. Steamboat

Top Resorts if you like hike-to terrain:
1. Aspen Highlands
2. Alta
3. Snowmass
4. Winter Park
5. Jackson Hole
6. Telluride

Top ski resorts if you are there for the food:
1. Deer Valley
2. Aspen
3. Telluride (especially for authentic Italian restaurants)

Top on-the-ski-mountain food:
1. Beaver Creek
2. Deer Valley

Top resorts for the nightlife:
1. Aspen
2. Vail

Top resorts if you are there for music:
1. Most free music courtesy of Bud Light and others = Vail and Aspen
2. Best Big name concerts in a ski town = Aspen
3. Best Blues = Winter Park

Top resorts if you are there for fun activities other than skiing:
1. Breckenridge: dogsledding, cross country skiing, snow shoeing
2. Beaver Creek: tubing, ice skating, theater, musical performances
3. Aspen: lectures, community and cultural events
4. Silver Mountain has Idaho's largest indoor water park

Top adaptive skiing resorts:
1. Winter Park
2. Sun Valley
3. Discovery Ski Area

Most family friendly large ski resorts:
1. Keystone
2. Sun Valley
3. Schweitzer Mountain Resort
4. Brighton because kids seven years old and under ski free.

Top resorts for your kids if you plan to ski primarily with your spouse:
1. Snowbird: Camp Snowbird, a state-licensed, fully staffed child-care center for children age six weeks to 12 years old, offers full day and half-day programs.
2. Keystone
3. Beaver Creek

Top twilight or night skiing:
1. Keystone is open 8:30 AM to 8:00 PM.
2. Schweitzer offers twilight skiing from 3:00 PM to 7:00 PM.
3. Brighton has night skiing on 200 acres including the main terrain park. There are three lifts open from 9:00 AM to 9:00 PM.
4. Park City offers twilight skiing from 4:00 PM to 8:00 PM.

Top Resorts for Snowboarding:
1. Keystone's terrain park is over 60 acres large and has over 100 features and a park specific lift.
2. Sun Valley is loved for its constant-pitch terrain.
3. Great Divide is "Montana's terrain park place."
4. Snowbasin, where the ski school teaches kids as young as three years old to snowboard.
5. Brighton has four parks and a pipe.
6. Whitefish has five terrain parks and a skier/boarder cross course.

Cheapest/best value passes:
1. Ski 2:30 – 4:30 at Alta. (It was only $38.)
2. The season pass at Winter Park offers a lot for the money.
3. The smaller mountains usually have the best prices, for example, Howelsen, Ski Cooper, Ski Grandby Ranch, Monarch, and Sunlight.
4. Snow King also offers a 2-hour ticket.

Top resorts if you like long runs:
1. Vail: The longest Run is Riva Ridge, which is four miles long.
2. Jackson Hole: The longest single run is either Gros Ventre or Sundance which both go from Bridger Gondola to the base. If you don't mind switching runs, the longest route is Rendevous Trail to Tram Line.

3. Big Sky: Although it's not a single run, Big Sky has a six mile route from Liberty Bowl to Mountain Mall. Take Liberty Bowl to Badlands to Hippy Highway to Cow Flats to Middle Road.

Best resorts for Catholics:
1. Beaver Creek, with ski-in, ski-out Mass
2. Alta. Our Lady of the Snows is located directly across from Alta Lodge. There is Catholic Mass every Sunday at 5:00 p.m. during the ski season.

Best resorts for Protestants:
1. Beaver Creek, with ski-in, ski-out church services
2. Winter Park has on-the-slopes services.

Best resort to be at for Christmas:
1. Aspen provides a "12 Days of Christmas" program.

These are my honest opinions. Occasionally, what I believe might not line up with a statistic. For example, Corbet's Couloir at Jackson Hole felt steeper than a run that is actually steeper somewhere else. If there is anything in this book that you believe is not consistent with statistics or perception, please let me know so that I can check it out thoroughly for a future edition of this book. I also welcome opinions because there is strength in consensus. You can email me at TheGuideJordanGale@yahoo.com. I'd love to hear anything that is true and honest without spin.

The ski industry is forever exciting. Back when I was writing the first edition of this book, Vail Mountain had just announced plans to replace the Avanti Express Lift in 2015 with a six-passenger lift. The then current chairlift was a detachable quad that was installed in 1989. Its maximum lift capacity was 2,800 people per hour. The new lift has increased capacity by about a third. Upgrading the lift reduced wait times and improved reliability. Vail Mountain has made six lift upgrades in the last seven years.

Resorts Getting Larger

What does the future hold? Will there someday be a way to connect the seven Salt Lake area ski resorts (Park City, Deer Valley, Canyons, Brighton, Solitude, Alta and Snowbird)? Many people are talking about the possibility. Utah launched a $1.8 million dollar marketing campaign to market the state as "Ski City USA." Steamboat, which calls itself "Ski Town USA" didn't like that idea very much at first. However, everyone has come to an agreement and Utah's Salt Lake City area is now being marketed as "Ski City."

Until 2013, Vail Mountain was the largest ski resort in America with over 3,000 skiable acres. However, in 2013, Montana's Big Sky Resort purchased Moonlight Basin and Spirit Mountain, giving it over 5,000 skiable acres. Now the combination of Park City and Canyons has made the Park City Mountain resort the largest resort, with over 7,000 skiable acres.

With ski areas getting bigger, lift lines getting shorter, and amenities getting better, what other great things are happening?

- ✓ Purgatory has a new lift and new trails.
- ✓ Snowbowl installed its first high-speed six-pack chairlift.
- ✓ Steamboat Ski Area started the planning for two new lifts and another gondola.
- ✓ Alta's proposed upgrade plan received initial approval.
- ✓ Taos Ski Valley now has the Blake hotel.
- ✓ Jackson Hole is building a new gondola.
- ✓ Big Sky is installing a six-seater bubble lift.

The first edition of this book had different improvements including:

- ✓ Idaho's Sun Valley Resort engaged in a large-scale tree-thinning project.
- ✓ Schweitzer Mountain Resort invested over $1 million dollars for a new grooming machine, upgraded snowmaking capabilities, new bathrooms, new ski and snowboard racks, and a newly paved parking lot.
- ✓ Lookout Pass made improvements and upgrades to three terrain parks.
- ✓ Brundage Mountain completed a major upgrade to its base lodge.
- ✓ A new ski resort called Cherry Creek

Ski resorts keep getting better in many different types of ways:

- ✓ Better lodges
- ✓ More tree-skiing terrain
- ✓ Better terrain parks
- ✓ Better snow grooming
- ✓ More snowmaking
- ✓ Better parking
- ✓ Faster chairlifts
- ✓ Shorter lift lines
- ✓ Better amenities
- ✓ More skiable acres

It's a great time to go to the best resorts we have ever had. They just keep getting better. Now the question is what to do there: ski, snowboard or both. That important question deserves thoughtful consideration. The next chapter provides information that should be considered before that decision is made.

13. Skiing and/or Snowboarding

A long time ago, there was only skiing. The ski industry grew over many decades. Skiing was expensive, yet that did not deter its growth. In the 1970s, the chairlifts were very slow. However, back then people were more patient and were so glad to get a ride up the hill that the slowness of the lift was of no concern. Back in the day, the clothes were not that warm. It was common to get cold, especially on the lifts. Yet being cold did not deter the skiers. In fact, skiers would boast about the days when they went out in negative five degrees Fahrenheit or negative fifteen degrees Fahrenheit or whatever degree they could boast about. Weathering the cold was thought to be part of the adventure, part of what made it cool, part of what made snow skiing so hard-core. Back then there was limited snowmaking and snow-grooming equipment. Therefore, snow conditions were less desirable. In spite of all these things, people loved to ski.

Then an odd thing happened. Skiing stalled. I never heard a good reason for why this happened, but it did. About that time, snowboarding was introduced, and snowboarding took off. Most snowboarders, in the early days, were kids or teenagers. Their interest in snowboarding helped keep ski resorts alive. Snowboarding became the cool thing to do. The snowboarding trend may be the last trend that you heard about, but if it is, there is more to know.

Snowboarding has not only stalled, but it is now on the decline. The Denver Post reported, "Snowboarding participation fell 4.5 percent during the last five years, while skiing grew 6.7 percent." (These statistics were provided by the National Ski Areas Association.) The Seattle Times reported that sales of snowboard equipment has declined 21% over the last four years, while the sales of skis climbed 3% during the same period. SnowSports Industries America informed us that skiing has replaced snowboarding as the most popular sport among kids ages 6-17. Taking a long-term view, the National Sporting Goods Association says that snowboard participation has dropped 22% since 2004, while skiing has climbed 16% during those years.

There is no single reason for these trends. This shift occurred due to a combination of reasons. One of the reasons may be that the word got out that learning to snowboard could be a little bit painful. It's not that there are a lot of injuries while learning to snowboard, it's that there can be a lot of falls. During the first few days on the snow, there are typically less falls learning to ski than learning to snowboard.

When I learned to snowboard, I felt like I was doing a belly flop off the high dive in the pool. It was painful, but I had no injuries from it. It took me four or five days of snowboarding with many painful falls before something clicked and falling became infrequent.

Another reason why some snowboarders made the switch is that cat tracks and flat terrain are easier to deal with on skis than on snowboards. There are sections on many mountains that snowboarders talk about in terms of "not getting stuck over there." If a snowboarder does not have enough speed to keep sliding through the flat section and their snowboard stops, then the rider is left with less desirable choices like jumping forward with the snowboard strapped to their feet until they get to the next section that slopes downward. Jumping is quite a workout. Another alternative is rocking back and forth with more force when rocking forward. Another alternative is taking one foot out of the snowboard and pushing off the snow with the foot that is out, kind of like skateboarding with a little resistance. Alternatively, a snowboarder sometimes feels the need to take both feet out of the snowboard and walk. Meanwhile, skiers easily skate or poll across the same terrain.

This leads us to a third reason why some people made the switch from snowboarding to skiing - there is a lot of time spent putting your snowboard on and taking it off. By contrast, once someone has his or her skis on, their equipment is usually in place until lunch.

All this being said, I still snowboard on some days. Back when I snowboarded on beginner terrain, I noticed that snowboarding doesn't use muscles in the same ways as skiing, and therefore I snowboarded once a week in order to give my skiing muscles a day of rest. When I became an intermediate snowboarder, I exerted more energy, so I no longer considered a day of snowboarding the equivalent of a day of rest. Although I had to take days of rest about once a week, I found that I liked to snowboard whenever I was in certain moods. If I was angry, tired, or mellow, I preferred to snowboard. Whenever I am feeling strong or happy, I prefer to ski.

Another benefit to doing both is that I can choose my equipment based on the person I am meeting on the mountain. If I am going to meet an expert skier or snowboarder, then I ski because I am much better at it. If I need to meet someone on the mountain who is a beginner or intermediate, then I grab my snowboard and go. Having both types of equipment gives me more options for any given day.

I know of some parents who told their kids they have to ski until they can ski expert terrain, then they can switch to snowboarding. When I asked why, I was told that when the adults are skiing, it's easier to keep the family together when everyone is skiing because then you don't have to stop as often and everyone moves at a faster pace.

Choosing Between Skiing or Snowboarding

If you have never skied or snowboarded before, and you can't decide whether to ski or snowboard, then (all other things being equal) I would recommend that you first try whichever your best friends do. The reason I say this is that snowboarders need to stop when they get off the lift and skiers tend to keep going when they get off the lift, so things flow more in sync when skiers ski together and snowboarders ride together. When mixed groups are together, a skier might have to gather a little patience at the top of the lift, while the snowboarder puts on his snowboard, and again at the bottom when he unstraps from one of his bindings. Conversely, a snowboarder might get a little frustrated with his skiing friend, if that person gives no thought to terrain that is not as appealing to snowboarders and leads his friend into flat terrain or moguls.

As a skier, moguls are my favorite place to be. I don't happen to know a single snowboarder who loves moguls. People who crave environments that require agility tend to love moguls.

For those of you who love speed, the groomed runs are the place to be and both skiers and snowboarders can enjoy the thrill of speed. However, at the professional level, the fastest skier goes faster than the fastest snowboarder. So to a racecar driver on the slopes for the first time, I would recommend skiing.

For those of you who love camaraderie, both skiing and snowboarding can provide it. However, I must admit that snowboarding in "the park" may offer the highest levels of camaraderie. Sometimes the entrance to a park looks like a party with so many people standing around socializing. On sunny spring days, the entrance to a park can look a little like the beach or a sporting event with people sitting in the sun chatting. The jumps and rails in the park also offer park riders the opportunity to talk about how to do various tricks. If you see a rider you'd like to get to know who is headed for the park, just follow, and whenever you both stop, it won't be hard to strike up a conversation by talking about how to do tricks.

You may be thinking that skiers can be in the park too, and that is true. I have been in the park many times. However, the ratio of snowboarders to skiers is much higher in the park. There have been many times when I looked around for a skier to ask a question about how to do a certain skiing trick and there was no one within earshot, even though snowboarders surrounded me.

Most people's feet naturally point straight ahead, but if your toes tend to point in a little bit, then your natural V shape might make skiing easier for you. Likewise, if your toes tend to point out like a ballerina doing a plié, then snowboarding might be more comfortable for you.

There are probably more generalizations that can be made to help first time people decide whether to snowboard or ski. If someone were a natural born show-off, then I would steer them towards snowboarding, where they can enjoy people standing around and watching their tricks. All other things being equal, if someone has very strong quadriceps from biking or other sports, I would steer them towards skiing. If someone is big into nature, I might steer him or her towards skiing with the thought that they might be the type of person who would enjoy hiking out of bounds once they have developed their skills.

If I was talking to a young child between six and ten years old, I would just ask them what they think they would prefer. Somehow, I think kids know what they will like most. If you are an adult and can imagine what your six-year-old self would enjoy more, then that might be the choice to make.

If you choose skiing, then the next chapter will help you navigate your way down mogul fields with confidence. If you choose snowboarding, then feel free to skip the next four pages, and pick up again on the topic that affects all of us: vacation planning.

14. Moguls

Top 10 Tips for Intermediate skiers in Moguls

If you are an intermediate skier, you have probably been in the moguls. I hope that you have taken a mogul class. If not, here are the key things to try to do:

1. Keep your upper body facing downhill. When turning, people have a tendency to let their upper body face the direction they are turning. Resist that. Your legs should be facing the way you are turning but your torso should be facing directly downhill at all times.

2. Absorb the bumps. Even when you are skiing the troughs between the moguls there are high sections and low sections. In the high section, you need to pull your legs up toward your chest. In the low, deep sections, you need to extend your legs. Absorbing the bumps is what will give you speed control. If you don't absorb the bumps, it is a matter of time before you get launched into the air.

3. Extend your legs in the deep sections of the troughs. Extending your legs will enable you to keep your skis on the snow. Once your skis are off the snow, you have less control. Keeping your skis on the snow gives maximum control. In addition to increasing control, extending your legs also gives

you optimal form. It gives the appearance of standing up straight in the valleys of the troughs.

4. Don't bend at the waist. For some reason, people have a tendency to bend at the waist when they get in the moguls. Bending forward at the waist is bad form.

5. Lean forward downhill. In my early days of skiing, I was told that if I lean back on my skis I will go faster, but if I lean forward downhill, I will go slower and have more control. I've been leaning forward ever since. The key to not falling is speed control. If you lean forward, you get more speed control.

6. Look a few moguls ahead. Professionals have told me that looking five moguls ahead is optimal. I can ski 200 yards of moguls without needing to leave my line and I usually look three or four moguls ahead. You'll find a place that is comfortable. The most important thing is not to look down at the snow right in front of you. If you do, you may end up sprawled out on that snow. Always look at the spot that you want to go to in a few turns.

7. When you start out on a mogul run, choose a good line. Choosing a good line can make the mogul experience so fun. How do you pick a good line? You want to look for troughs that are evenly spaced and are very consistent as they go in a zigzag line down the mountain.

8. Keep your hands in front of you as if you are carrying a cafeteria tray. Do not let one hand drop as you make a turn. Do not swing your arms. (The only place swinging your arms is acceptable is deep powder.) Your hands should always be facing directly downhill because your upper body is always facing directly downhill. If you notice that your invisible cafeteria tray in your hands faces the side of the slope as you turn, then bring your hands back to facing downhill.

9. You plant your pole and go around it, just like when you ski anywhere else on the mountain. This is done with a small wrist action to bring the pole forward to plant it. Do not

make any drastic actions in order to plant your pole. Your hand should appear still from a distance even though your wrists are flicking the poles forward.

10.   Breathe. Believe it or not, some people hold their breath when they start out on a mogul field. You need oxygen more than ever in moguls, so remember to breathe.

Beyond these tips, it is practice, practice, practice that will get you skiing down the moguls with ease. Some things are easy to learn and some things take time. Moguls take time.

As you practice the moguls, you will know when you get it right. From that point, you can start to develop some "muscle memory" of how your body should behave in the moguls. Even once you can finally go through the moguls with ease, take the time to think about each of the above tips for a long section, just to make sure you haven't developed any bad habits. The tips above will help you ski the moguls most efficiently, which means you can ski more of them without getting tired. It also means that you can get through the moguls with less effort than your friend who is skiing less efficiently.

Often people ask what part of the moguls to ski. The answer is that you can ski any part of them. The best place to learn to ski the moguls is the troughs. This will keep you in a path downward. As you progress, you can ski the top sides or the bottom sides of the moguls; it doesn't really matter. Skiing the very top, or the tips, of the moguls is mostly for people who want to race through the moguls really fast. Don't try that until you can take a path straight down between two sets of moguls. If you need to traverse moguls in order to make it down, then you are not yet ready to try skiing the tops.

Speaking of traversing, there is an excellent drill for moguls to practice absorbing and extending. To do it, you traverse the entire width of the mogul field, while thinking about extending your legs in the deep part of the troughs and absorbing the high parts by bringing your knees to your chest. The reason that this is such a good drill is that you don't have to worry about gaining speed because you are not heading downhill. This frees your mind to process the timing of extending and absorbing. It also enables you to focus on keeping your skis on the snow as the snow goes up and down.

Getting good in the moguls has the nice benefit of getting hooted and hollered at from the chairlifts. People love to watch skilled mogul skiers.

One more thing about moguls, keep your knees together and your skis close together. Your stance is closest together in the moguls, more natural in powder, a little farther apart on groomed runs and farthest apart in crud.

15. Vacation Planning

Skiing is sometimes perceived as a sport for the wealthy because a one-day ski ticket costs more than many activities. However, if someone wants to ski, it can be done, no matter what your budget is.

If you have a lot of money and don't mind spending it, then all you need to do is give your assistant some direction on what type of place to get. If you can answer these questions, it will help you get what you want:

1. Which resort do you want to go to? If you know which resort you want to go to, that narrows things down a lot. If you don't know which resort you want to go to, but you know attributes of the ski mountain that you want to go to (such as powder versus wet snow, steeps versus moguls, night life or family friendly, snowboarding versus skiing, or other attributes of mountains that are described in this book), you can have your assistant read those chapters and make decisions based upon the criteria that is important to you. Alternatively, you can let the remainder of these questions determine the best vacation spot for you.

2. Do you want a ski-in/ski-out accommodation, or is a larger accommodation with a driver who will bring you to the mountain just as good?

3. How many bedrooms and how many bathrooms do you want?

4. What are your dates? Are your dates flexible?

5. Do you want to provide an approximate budget?

6. Are there any amenities that are important to you? Examples include indoor hot tub, outdoor hot tub, pool, fitness center, or business center?

7. Do you prefer to be in town where you can walk to restaurants and activities? Or do you prefer to be in a quiet location, where you won't hear noise late at night?

8. Are there any other attributes that are important to you? I know people who feel it is important to have a washer and dryer in the accommodation. Is there a minimum square footage that is important to you? Most rentals come with free Internet but if that is important to you, your assistant had better confirm it.

If you are an average American with an average budget, you will want to answer most of the questions above. The main difference is that you will have to find your rental yourself. There are several ways to do it.

The fastest, easiest way to get a reservation is to pick the resort, go to their website, click on lodging, look around at the options, call the 800 number on the site to ask any questions and make the booking.

Another way to do it, which might save you a little bit of money is go to web sites where owners rent to you directly. The site that I have used the most often is vrbo.com. VRBO stands for Vacation Rental By Owner. There are also other popular sites like homeaway.com and flipkey.com.

Many of the above web sites offer attributes that discourage scams. For example, when a person has to pay money to be on a web site, it discourages some scammers. When the website offers vacation insurance and will reimburse you if there is a scammer online, then the site is proactive about removing scammers from their website.

If you want to save even more money, then Craigslist may be your choice. I put this in a category by itself because it is different from other websites. I have rented a wonderful ski-in ski-out condo in Telluride's Mountain Village through Craigslist. I must admit that as I was driving there, I was hoping that the person to whom I already paid $2,000 was legitimate. I had done some checking like whether the name on the tax record for that property matched the name that I was asked to make the check out to. However I still didn't completely trust the purchase was legitimate. Too much of the drive there was filled with the same thought, "I hope the condo will be there when I get there. I hope the condo will be there when I get there. I hope the condo will be there when I get there." The good news is that it was there and I was very happy with the condo. It was even nicer than I expected because they had just put in new carpeting, fresh paint, and all the kitchen utensils that I needed.

Payment for a vacation rental is not the same as a hotel rental. Vacation rentals often require large portions of the rental amount in advance. Sometimes it is upon booking. Other times it is 60 days before arrival.

Of course you can always rent a hotel room. If you have frequent stayer points, then that hotel chain would be the place to start to see what ski resorts they have hotels at. On the other hand, if you are firm on the resort that you want, then you can Google "hotels in Vail", or whichever ski resort you want to go to. When I did that, I immediately saw a list and noticed that there is a Holiday Inn and a Marriot (if I want to go with a hotel chain I am familiar with), as well as several independent hotels that look like they have great amenities to offer.

After I have my travel arrangements, my mind usually shifts to Gear. What gear should I put on my Christmas list? What gear should I look for before I get to the mountain? What gear should I wait to get until I am there?

16. Gear

A lot of people recommend renting skis, boots and poles when you first start to learn to ski. I suppose it is a wise recommendation, if you are only planning to ski a few days or less per year.

If you are planning to ski a week or more each season, then you might prefer to get your own equipment. A benefit of having your own equipment is that it is the same every time you ski. It is easier to start where you left off when the equipment is the same. When you change equipment each time, it might feel a little different.

I think the most important gear is your clothes. Dressing for the temperature will greatly increase your enjoyment of being outside. Most beginners err on the side of not dressing warm enough. Feel free to layer. You can always take a layer of clothes off in the lodge and leave it there until the end of the day if you get too warm.

Fashion is fun, however if you are buying cold weather clothes, I am of the opinion that function is a little more important than style. If you can have both, that is all the better. However, sometimes trade-offs are necessary. In the long run, I will love warm gloves more than stylish gloves. A warm coat will let me stay outside longer than a stylish coat. In terms of style, almost anything goes at a ski resort. Back before Gore-Tex jackets, skiers would wear large garbage bags if it rained. Skiers understand the need for appropriate clothing and warmth.

The features in the skis, boots and poles that a skier chooses are important and helpful for optimum performance, which reminds me of a story I heard about Cubco Bindings.

Brandon said, "I've got a great ski story. This is old equipment. Do you remember the Cubco bindings? The Cubco binding was the poor man's version of the Look binding. The Look was the first step in bindings and the Cubco was the poor man's version that common people could afford. There was a single spring in the front and a single spring in the back with a pulley. The front you could release in any direction. And they hadn't figured out yet that you needed plates underneath your boot. This is before they knew that.

So my brother goes to the Cunjamuck jump. It's a big rock, so he goes off the Cunjamuck jump and he got ten feet in the air and both skis come off in mid-air because that's what happens. As you compress the ski, there's no problem because the Cubco bindings stay on because as you can imagine, they are getting tighter in the front and so it stays on. But then when it releases, the bottom of the ski pops up and hits the bottom of the boot in the rebound. So as you jump, it comes off. The skis just fall off, so every time you were skiing a mogul field with something like that, the skis would just fall off in mid air. You'd see like a cartoon character who is in mid air, his legs are pumping, he's got the safety straps on, so the skis are going to whack him. Remember the safety straps? They caused the ski to hit in the back of the head. And you knew that was all coming. I was just loving watching that. It was a classic."

I remember when I heard Brandon tell that story, I laughed because I could imagine it. His story reinforces the point that ski equipment is continually getting better and better. We no longer have to worry about our skis coming off, or about safety straps that would sometimes force our skis to hit us.

If garage sale equipment is all you can get, then by all means start with what you have to start with. You'll still have fun. But my recommendation is: "If you can afford to buy or rent equipment, you will be better off."

When deciding on equipment, choosing the right size is paramount. Proper fit is essential. Boots should be snug, but not tight. You do not want your big toe pressing up against the front of the boot.

If you put your pole upside down, touching the ground, and your hand immediately under the round basket of the pole, if your forearm is parallel to the ground, then you found the right size pole. A pole that is too long can cause you to ski leaning back, which will give you less speed control. A pole that is too short can give you bad form by causing you to bend at the waist in order to make the pole reach the snow.

A salesperson can help you choose skis that are the right length. Beginner skis are usually less expensive than expert skis, so don't bother to spend extra money early on when you don't ski like an expert. Web sites like REI.com often show recommended weights for different ski lengths. If you rent skis at first, then you can try different lengths to see what your favorite length is.

When I bought my first snowboard, I let the salesperson guide me. It worked out great. Knowledgeable salespeople who are good at communicating are invaluable. This season I'll plan to keep my eye out for demo days that some resorts and some shops offer. I love to demo equipment and feel the differences in how some skis and snowboards like long, carving turns, while others encourage me to take frequent, short radius turns.

To cooperate with the weather, this year I put long underwear tops on my Christmas list, and sent my family a couple of links to tops that offered high performance warmth and wicking, as well as a good look. I think my family notices that getting out on the slopes is good for my attitude, so I'm guessing I'll get the clothes I hoped for.

I recently purchased three neck gaiters online to be certain I got the kind I like. I am picky about those. Hint: fog free neck gators are the best for people like me who like to keep their nose and cheeks warm and dry.

Not everyone gives thought to wearing optimal clothing outdoors, but what is worse than that is never getting outdoors. Our youngest generation is getting outside less than any other generation and that is where the next chapter begins.

17. Nature

Psychologists are beginning to talk about Nature Deficit Disorder. Not many people talked about it ten years ago, but now it has become a big topic within certain circles. Nature deficit disorder refers to a hypothesis that children are spending less time outdoors, and that this change in culture is resulting in a wide range of behavioral problems. The disorder is not yet included in medical manuals for mental disorders, but it has been reviewed, and interest in the validity of the problem is causing more focus on this issue.

Evidence that kids are spending less time in nature is not hard to find. Consumption of electronic media by children is increasing. Those of you who have kids really don't need the statistics; you see it every day. Your kids don't spend their free time the way that you did at their age. There are some advantages of this change; often kids know how to use a computer better than their grandparents. However, it's clear there are big disadvantages to this shift indoors. The lure of electronic media didn't exist 20 years ago as it does today. Video games and apps have reached a new level. Kids are getting Internet access younger and younger. I know a six year old who has created a channel on YouTube.

Sedentary lifestyle has contributed to numerous health problems affecting children, especially childhood obesity. The negative effects of increased use of technologies can be mitigated. In addition to burning more calories, studies show that time in nature fosters creativity and calms children struggling with information overload.

The best-selling book, "Last Child in the Woods: Saving Our Children from Nature-Deficit Disorder" makes a strong case for how nature's restorative qualities can enliven creativity, reduce stress and attention deficit disorder, and give busy families a sense of rebalance and connection. This book sparked discussion that spawned a movement to reconnect kids and nature.

It's not only children who benefit from time in nature; it's good for adults too. The author of "The Nature Principle" wrote a book about how nature can boost mental acuity and creativity, promote health and wellness, build smarter and more sustainable businesses and communities, and ultimately strengthen human bonds.

There are many ways to get out into nature. Hiking, rafting, and camping are a few good ways. In the winter, it is more difficult to enjoy nature. However, skiing and snowboarding in the winter provides just that outlet, to allow us to enjoy nature in all its winter beauty.

In an interview with National Public Radio, author Richard Louv said, "Researchers at the University of Illinois are investigating whether time in the woods could be used to supplement treatment of ADD. A study at the University of Kansas found that young people who backpacked for three days showed higher creativity and cognitive abilities. People in hospitals that can see a natural landscape usually get better faster. As an antidote to nature deficit disorder, we need to figure out ways to increase nature time even as technology increases. It has to be a conscious decision."

Have you heard the phrase "sitting is the new smoking"? There is now evidence that shows that sitting long hours every day can have serious health risks similar to those caused by smoking.

You have a decision to make on how to spend this weekend. Consider getting out in nature. Decide to head to a ski mountain.

18. The Radical Life in Ski Towns

During the ten seasons that I have lived at seven ski resorts, I have found that ski towns, with the exception of Utah ski towns, are usually not very religious places. The remnants of devout people in those towns are often a tiny minority; sometimes they are a small group of 50 or 100 living amongst a thousand or two thousand people with different worldviews. I've met a few atheists in ski towns, but they are even fewer than the Catholics or the Protestants. Probably the local people I met most often in ski towns were people who have given less thought to religious matters than the average person. Many people have stories of moving to ski towns when they were in their early 20s. Some moved there to ski, others moved there to party, others to get away from the home life they grew up with, and in some cases, all of the above was the motivation. Living in a resort town provides a different subculture than most of America is accustomed to.

There is more pleasure to be found in a ski town than in most places, including but not limited to great food, lots of laughing, great fun, and a less strict moral code. Life in a ski town can be pleasurable from many different angles. It is not all out hedonism, but if you are looking for illicit pleasure, it is not hard to find at a ski resort.

If you are looking for something deeper, perhaps meaning, or calling, or purpose, or truth, those too can be found in a ski town. I have been impressed with how some people shine bright. Those who are seeking after God in the middle of resort life often show great love, sincere compassion, and ambition for things that matter.

Whenever I traveled to a ski town, I sought out a church. Every church that I ever attended in a ski town was very welcoming. The people at these gatherings are used to the ebb and flow of seasonal people and vacationing people attending their services, and they do a nice job of making visitors feel comfortable.

In Winter Park, Colorado, I heard about a church service that was held on one of the ski slopes. This was an intriguing idea to me. What a great idea to hold the service right where I wanted to be. They kept the service short, which I was glad about on cold days. Even in its brevity, there would almost always be good food for thought and wisdom for living life well. It was a nice location. People would sit on their snowboards or skis, or directly on the snow, overlooking a cross that was stuck in the ground, with the mountains in the background. You might want to try this church for the practical words of wisdom to help live life to the fullest.

In Beaver Creek, Colorado, there is a ski-in, ski-out chapel that several different churches use at different times of day. I picked the service where I could ski a couple of runs and then ski down to church. The people there really cared for each other, and for newcomers. Taking an hour off from skiing to feel community and caring was a highlight of my weekends. You might want to try this church for the sense of community.

In Telluride, Colorado, the church I went to met in the movie theater on Sunday mornings. Early on, I found out that they were looking for a drummer, and even though I was a novice at drumming, they included me in the music. I loved going to practice and working on the songs. My Roland electronic drum kit made it easy for the sound guy to lower my volume whenever necessary to make sure that everyone had a good time at church. I was struck with the sincerity of the people there. There was a genuineness that was very attractive. They were open in their conversations; interactions there were free from pretense. They had been praying for a drummer to join them and when I showed up on the scene, instead of focusing on the thought that they probably should have been praying for a highly skilled drummer, they were grateful for whatever God seemed to be providing. The church in Telluride may have been the smallest church I ever attended, but the vocalist who led the singing had one of the most beautiful voices I have ever heard. Every song was in her range, and the beauty of the sound sometimes brought tears to my eyes. Seldom do I hear any sound that beautiful. You might want to try this church for the beauty of the singing and for the refreshment of interacting with people who are kind and genuine.

In Aspen, Colorado, there is an unusual subculture because the rich seem richer and the poor seem poorer than at other resorts. After getting a feel for the Aspenites, I wondered what church would be like in this kind of unique town. The church there emphasized the importance of hearing God through reading the Bible. The Bible is God's instruction manual for living the most satisfying life possible. Sometimes the path to living a fulfilling life is not intuitive and the instruction from the Bible was very useful. Whether you are rich or poor, try this church if you are looking to live life in a better way than you have been living it in the past.

In Whistler, Canada, the church I went to left enough time to ski all day and catch a quick happy hour before heading to church. The convenient 4:30 start time and the location in the village, just a short walk from the gondolas, was convenient, but it was not the convenience that drew me back each week. Every week, the congregation prayed for forgiveness. There was humility and acknowledgment of the wrong things we had done and the good things we hadn't gotten around to. Every week, the congregation prayed for the local politicians and for the community. They really care about the people in their town, whether they believe in God or not. When there wasn't much snow, the congregation prayed for snow. When a local bar was the venue for a fundraiser and hair-cutting event to help cancer patients, the church prayed for that event, and supported the event in multiple ways. This church, which is technically Baptist, has a Pentecostal pastor, an Anglican style of prayer, and attenders from non-denominational and Catholic backgrounds. The church has locals from Canada, seasonal folks from Australia, and visitors from America and several other countries. The diversity isn't the main identity of the church. The strength in this church is the oneness among so many different types of people.

I skied a few days with a guy from church. He was in Whistler for the season from Germany. He had a Catholic background. He told me that when he went to this church for the first time, he was a little afraid when he saw a big guy with tattoos up front during announcement time. That didn't mesh with his expectations of church. However, he said he returned time after time because he also saw that there was a reverence for God when people worshipped that was touching. Other people were growing closer to God at this church, and he wanted to do that too.

This church in Whistler was also an offshoot for the Whistler Snowboarders for Christ group. Snowboarders and skiers met twice a week. I skied with them on Mondays. We would meet early at Starbucks and talk about yesterday's sermon, or hear a short devotional or something cool that someone had learned that week. Occasionally I would ask questions and I received thoughtful answers from multiple people in the group. What really impressed me though was when we hit the slopes. In a ski town where so many people only want to ski with people of their own level, who like the same types of terrain, with no more than three other people because chairlifts usually only seat four, we would sometimes have big groups and the most skilled were patient with the less skilled. The topic came up one day and one of the guys said, "Yeah, who would have thought that being Christ-like on the slopes would be better than being selfish and getting more of the runs I want? Who would've thought that this is better, but it is."

People who were trying to follow Jesus acted different than all the others who could care less, and that difference made a deep impression on me. A small candle looks bright when it is very dark out. It's intriguing; I want to meet more of these Jesus followers. I guess I could meet them anywhere, but I am looking forward to meeting more of them in the next ski town that I go to, wherever that might be.

19. Encouragement for Beginners

This chapter is for those who are new to skiing, because we all start as novices. If you are an intermediate or an expert, there may be some miscellaneous tidbits that you find useful, or you may want to read this so that you can pass this chapter on to a friend or someone you love who you are encouraging to join you for fun times on the slopes.

Expectations have a lot to do with enjoying life. If we expect too much, we might be disappointed, even with something wonderful. Remember that even ski resorts are part of reality, and struggle is part of the human plight. Skiing is not easy, but it is not hard either. That is, skiing is not hard if you have the right attitude.

Therefore, I recommend that you expect to fall. It may or may not happen, but if you know that it may happen, and that the consequences are not dire, then there is no need to worry about falling. Remember when we were kids. We really wanted a bike for Christmas and then once we got the bike, we really wanted to know how to ride it. We weren't concerned about the possibility of falling. Our egos had not yet gotten that big. Skiing brings us all back to that child-like state of wanting to do something and not knowing how to do it. It has the excitement of envisioning success, and the setbacks of miscalculations in balance.

Please don't exaggerate the risk of skiing in your mind. Some people blow up the fear of getting hurt, so large, until they are paralyzed and can do nothing. What good is having a well functioning body, if you choose not to enjoy the activities that a healthy body enables you to enjoy? I'm guessing that when you got in the car yesterday, you put your physical safety in more danger than you will by skiing tomorrow. So in reality, the fear is unjustified.

As you know, if you expect too much, you might be disappointed. Likewise, if you expect too little you might not experience the excitement. Skiing can be filled with experiences of wonder. From the enjoyment of a beautiful view at a peak, to the serendipity of the feeling of flying through the air and landing softly, childlike wonder can be felt in many ways while on a mountain.

Another great aspect of skiing is the camaraderie and appreciating the people that you are with. There is a feeling of togetherness riding the chairlift, chatting during the gondola ride, following your friends down the hill, and heading into the lodge for lunch with huge appetites and great stories. You are together, and there are no distractions.

If you are the beginner, realize that it is OK to be a novice. It is temporary. Most people would agree that it is good to keep learning. If you agree that it is good to keep learning things, then give yourself some kudos for learning to ski.

The views and spending time with people may be the easiest benefits to explain, but they are not the best benefits. For those of you who are religious, you may consider trying to be in the frame of mind to worship. You might want to hum a song, or think a prayer. The typical religious activities done in the natural environment feel different than those same activities inside a church building. Singing, praying, and meditating, while noticing nature, are good at the deepest level because God reveals himself through nature.

There is even more - the unexplainable part. The peace that surpasses understanding. The joy that feels like it is overflowing. It is amazing to feel the wonder of God revealing himself through nature. You can easily miss it. Prepare your heart to take it in. Ask God to reveal Himself. Quiet your mind to hear it. Seek it out. Nothing is more worthy of a search.

The hardest benefit to articulate is the "I don't know what that feeling is" that is experienced by so many on the slopes. It's the feeling of moguls, in rhythm, underneath your body. It is so pleasurable that it just doesn't make sense. Or feeling the poetry of carving skis on a freshly groomed run; there are experiences that cannot be put into words. These experiences will probably not occur on your first day. However, if you are open to experiencing amazing things that you have never experienced before, I would be surprised if you don't experience wonderful things that you esteem with extreme appreciation.

Another great thing about skiing is how it is so easy to live in the moment while on the slopes. Issues at work feel a million miles away. Relationships with family feel smoother. Friends feel closer. Concerns about the future melt on the side of the mountain. Politics and world events are nonexistent. When living in the moment, all is right in the world.

Skiers, who focus on skiing and forget about the other aspects of their lives while on the slopes, get a great escape from the ordinariness of life and many say the result is increased happiness. That totally immersed, engaged feeling has a positive effect on one's sense of well-being.

Skiing is a healthy activity. It burns calories and strengthens muscles. Look around at a ski resort; you don't see many unfit people there. I've read that you can burn 3,000 calories in six hours of skiing. So for some people, that can mean weight loss. For other people it means guilt-free multi-course meals. The best thing about burning those calories is that most of us never give it a thought while we are on the slopes. Strict diets can be hard to follow and hard exercise in a fitness center can feel like work, but skiing the calories away feels like vacation.

Skiing uses your core, which is the section of your body between your legs and your arms. Strong stomach muscles are a great benefit of skiing. However, the only muscles I hear people talking about on the chairlift are their quadriceps. Skiing gives a great workout to thigh muscles. Using one's poles on flat sections of snow, increases arm strength, so skiing is a great overall body workout.

If you want to prepare for the physical exertion, biking is a great way to get in shape for skiing. However, if exercising is not really your thing, you can sit against a wall for a couple of minutes a day. In this position, your calves are vertical and your thighs are horizontal and your back is against the wall; as if you are sitting in a chair against the wall, but there is no chair. This exercise targets the muscles in your thighs, which could prevent you from getting sore from over-exertion on your vacation.

Skiing also provides cardiovascular exercise. How much of a cardiovascular workout is attained while skiing, varies from skier to skier. However, most skiers do elevate their heart rates at various times during the day.

The thing I love about skiing is that I get a great workout and I don't even notice that I am exercising. In contrast, exercise like cycling and running, tempt my mind to think about the work involved. When I am skiing, I don't even notice the exercise because my mind is engrossed in the fun I am having.

Like most exercise, skiing is great for reducing stress and helping people get a better night of sleep. It's not just the exercise that is good for a person's stress level, the chairlift rides are a great time for socializing, and so many topics are discussed that might not ordinarily be approached. I've also heard of one person refer to the chairlift rides as "therapy."

For those of us who like to exercise our brains, skiing is great for that. The brain is very active, feeling various body positions and movements. Many skiers talk of "muscle memory", but what they really mean is that the brain remembers exactly how your muscles should be at various points.

Skiing is also a great way to get out into the sunshine. For people who seasonally suffer depression during the winters and are in need of getting enough sunlight, skiing is a great way to be outdoors for hours at a time.

For those of you who believe in mental health days, I'm sure that you will find that skiing enhances your mental health. Skiing helps to clear your mind, get rid of anger, and begin thinking about problems in a new way. A day on the mountain changes a person.

Behavioral psychologists have found that skiing makes people happier. A study was done at ski resorts in South Korea, and the findings are interesting. They purport that the focus and "flow" that skiing requires increases happiness. They further show that although skiing and snowboarding both increase happiness, skiing increases happiness the most.

The Learning Process

No discussion for the beginner would be advantageous without some advice on the learning process. Of course, lessons are extremely beneficial. If you can afford to take lessons from a professional, then you are very fortunate. I started skiing when I was twelve years old, and I took a lesson every time I went skiing with the school's ski club. I am now an expert skier, and whenever I can, I do like to take lessons.

I was especially impressed with the programs at Taos, Breckenridge Ski Resort and Telluride. I had a Breckenridge Ski School Lesson Pass (for season pass holders) that gave me many lessons. The lessons at Breckenridge helped to improve my technique and kept me from developing bad habits. Likewise, I had a limitless lesson pass the season I was at Telluride, and I still remember specific tips that I apply to my skiing today to make me a better skier. No one is too good for lessons. A beginner might not realize it at first, but lessons are very beneficial.

One of the many benefits of taking lessons is that it can make you a more efficient skier. If you learn the proper way to ski, you will be able to easily ski the terrain that others are struggling to get through. Since skiing is a very physical sport, efficient skiers last longer in the day, and can ski more days in a row.

Another benefit of taking lessons is that learning the optimal way to get down the hill can prevent injuries. Too many "hot dogs" who feel they are awesome at everything they do, even on the first try, point their skis straight down hill, only to gain too much speed as they are headed towards the bottom, which is a recipe for a spectacular crash. Skiing is all about speed control. Even the fastest skiers know that they should only ski as fast as they can ski while under control. Lessons can teach you how to control your speed.

If you feel a little bit of "hot dog" in you, please remember that even the Olympic skiers have coaches that give instructions. Even ski instructors have instructors. Instruction is meant for those who hope to be great skiers.

It is very pleasant to take lessons. It is easier to do the unknown, when there is someone there to break things down into baby steps. Rather than guess at it, or trust a friend who doesn't look anything like the skiers you see on television, a professional ski instructor knows what you should be doing and can recommend what to focus on first in order to speed your progress. The fastest way to get good at skiing is to learn from the professionals.

The other people in the class will be your same level, so if you have never skied before, you will be put in a class with other beginners. At any level, all things being equal, it is more fun to ski with people who are the same level, not better or worse. Skiers of the same level usually ski at similar speeds, so there are no excessively long waits at the bottom of the hill waiting for the slower skiers. Sometimes people who meet in a class decide to ski together later in the week, to enjoy new friendships and enjoy the skiing compatibility of skiers who are at the same level.

Private lessons are great too, but in a different way. You get to go to the type of terrain that you love most and the instructor focuses totally on improving your skiing. The drills are selected carefully with a particular purpose in mind to bring your skills to the next level.

There was a funny advertisement that read something like "Save a relationship; take a lesson." People would laugh at it, but no one outright disagreed with it. If you are a beginner, please realize that it might be hard for someone who is very good at skiing to be patient enough to go as slow as a beginner goes. It also might be hard for a more advanced skier to choose to go on the easiest slopes, which is where beginners belong, when they are longing to go on terrain that is commensurate with their skill level. Although some people enjoy teaching other people, most skiers would rather be skiing their own terrain at their own speed. If a friend offers to teach you, and you accept, be aware of whether you reach a point where their patience is being tried. If the teacher/friend gives you some information and watches you attempt the skills, don't be surprised if your friend wants to leave you on the "bunny" slope to head to something more challenging while you practice.

Practice is necessary. A lot of skiing is spending the hours on the slope required to get good at it. Time spent does translate to improved skill level.

Aside from being a challenge for the teacher/friend, the dynamic can also be challenging on a student/friend. Some people find it easier to take direction from a professional than a friend. More commonly, it is difficult for a relationship of equals in friendship to make the switch to the teacher-student roles. A friend might unintentionally sound condescending as they try to help you improve. When you are used to having a friendship of equals, it might be difficult to hear your friend talk like a know-it-all. Even when you know that your friend knows more than you, sometimes it is just hard on emotions to change the typical dynamic of a relationship.

Here are the levels of skiing:

Level one is the true beginner who is trying skiing for the first time. The most important thing to learn right away is how to stop. At level one, skiers and riders are making their first turns.

Level two usually describes people who have spent a day or two on the slopes. Level two skiers are comfortable putting on their equipment and have learned how to glide and stop on the easiest learning terrain. Level two skiers are working on improving their turns.

Level three skiers are comfortable making turns on beginner terrain and are now working on the transition from "wedge turns" to "parallel turns." Level three skiers are also working on being able to make different size turns, and developing a rhythm in skiing.

Level four skiers can ski all "green circle" terrain. Ski runs marked with green circles are considered beginner ski runs. Skiers on these slopes are working on linking smooth, gliding turns. Skiers may position their skis parallel to each other some of the time, but probably use a slight wedge more of the time, especially when the hill gets a little steeper

Level five skiers have progressed from "green circle" runs to "blue square" runs. The blue square symbol indicates that a run is for skiers of intermediate skiing ability. Level five skiers might be working on learning how to use their poles for better timing and precision.

Level six skiers are confident on groomed "blue square" terrain and are capable of skiing the easiest ungroomed and mogul-filled blue terrain. Level six skiers are working to learn to use both skis independently.

Level seven skiers have ventured from the "blue square" terrain to the easier "black diamond" slopes. Black diamond slopes are considered expert terrain. Level seven skiers are working on managing higher speeds under control. Level seven skiers begin to enjoy the whole mountain, including moguls, steeps, powder, racing, carving, crud, ice and freestyle runs.

Level eight skiers have confidence on most terrain and are now working on refining techniques for efficiency.

Level nine skiers can ski almost anywhere. These skiers have developed confidence and flair. They are efficient in their movements. The next step for level nine skiers is to have that same confidence on "double-black diamond" runs.

As you progress through the levels of skiing, take your time and enjoy the activity. People who try to skip from one level to the next without working on the skills of their level usually end up not having very good form.

In the early stages of skiing, it is recommended that skiers keep their skis in a "pizza slice" position. Later, skiers develop into the "french fry" position. You learn things in the "pizza" position that help you do the "french fry" position properly. If you learn things in order, and don't try to skip ahead, you will be better off.

You have probably heard the phrase "repetition is the mother of all learning." This axiom is true of skiing. The more you repeat what you learn, the more comfortable it will get and the more ready for the next step you will be.

Types of Terrain

From an earlier section, you now know that "green circles" indicate beginner terrain, "blue squares" indicate intermediate terrain, "black diamonds" indicate expert terrain, and "double black diamonds" are for the hardcore experts. If you haven't been to a ski resort yet, double black diamonds are graphically represented by two black diamonds next to each other (not a dark shade of black).

Groomed runs refer to those trails that a big machine that looks part tractor and part tank have been on recently. Groomers smooth the snow. The snow looks a little bit like a beach that was recently raked. The grooves in the snow make it look like corduroy. If you are a beginner, it is a good idea to look at the grooming report to see if any green circle runs have been groomed. Groomed snow makes things a little easier, so head towards the groomed runs.

People who like to go fast usually like groomed runs, but the speedsters will most likely be on intermediate groomed runs. The pitch of the intermediate runs makes getting a lot of speed possible. People who like to go fast on groomed runs will likely be "carving" which means that they tilt their skis on edge to minimize skidding and maximize deep, precise turns. The smooth snow is preferable to unsmooth snow for the same reason you would rather go 55 miles per hour on a paved highway than on a bumpy dirt road.

Another group of people, unrelated to the people who love speed, are the people who love powder. Powder is soft, dry snow. Advanced skiers like deep powder because it is soft to ski on. It is possible to feel like you are floating when you ski powder. Utah is known for its very dry snow and is referred to as champagne powder.

You may hear people talk about a run that has crud on it. This is a description, not a defamation of the run. The snow is an uneven surface, usually with some soft and some hard lumps of snow. Therefore, the amount of resistance that your skis encounter is frequently changing. Skiing on crud can be challenging, but the key is to ski more aggressively. In addition, focusing on where you are going and choosing your way through the terrain on the less bumpy areas will make the run a little easier.

If someone doesn't know your skiing ability and asks if you want to join them when they ski the back bowls or ski the glades, all beginners should just say "No." Bowls are areas above the tree line that are wide open, and flow down on three sides. (You can imagine a cereal bowl that someone drops at breakfast and one side comes off of it.) Bowls often have moguls, which are mounds of snow. When people first learn to ski moguls, they usually learn to ski in the troughs between the bumps in the snow. Later they learn to ski the tops or the upper sides or the lower sides of the bumps.

Glade skiing is skiing between lots of trees. Generally people learn to ski moguls first, where they learn to make turns around the bumps in the snow. Later, they progress to making turns around trees. Whether the obstacle is a mound of snow or a tree, learning to control your skis so that they do what you want them to do is fun.

As a beginner, you won't be near any cornices, but just so that you know what it means when you hear the stories of your expert buddies... a cornice is an overhang of snow on a ridge. The shape is caused by the wind. It looks a little bit like an ocean wave that has curved up into the shape of the letter C before the wave breaks.

Another word that is handy to know is "knoll." A knoll is a small rounded hill. If someone says ski past that knoll and you will reach a cat track that will take you to the lift, then look for a small rounded hill to ski by so that you can reach the flat, skinny path that will lead to the chairlift.

In order to understand more skiing terms, there is a glossary at the end of this book. Knowing the lingo will help you more clearly communicate with other skiers and riders. How many of the words and phrases in the glossary do you know? Before you turn to the glossary, there is a short message from the author for you to read.

20. Message from the Author

I hope that this book was helpful to you and that you enjoyed it. Thank you for reading it.

There are so many resorts with so many different strengths, personalities and subcultures. Each resort is important for the good it does in its community and for the good it does by helping people vacation, enjoy nature and connect with loved ones.

Writing this book has reminded me of times that made me smile and giggle and feel glad to be alive. I hope this book has inspired you to venture to resorts that you haven't been to yet, and to appreciate your favorite resorts.

If you would like to suggest any modifications or additions to the third edition of this book, feel free to email me at TheGuideJordanGale@yahoo.com.

Happy skiing.

Jordan Gale

Glossary

Alpine skiing = downhill skiing. (Not Nordic skiing, which is cross-country skiing on relatively flat terrain).

Après ski = after skiing. (After skiing, a lot of skiers go to get a drink and/or a snack together to socialize before going home.)

Avalanche beacon = an electronic device that expert skiers bring with them when they go out of bounds. If there is an avalanche, it helps the non-buried skiers to find their friends who are buried under the snow.

Avalanche control = the triggering of avalanches in order to make the inbound slopes safe for skiers. Explosions are often used for avalanche control.

Backcountry = the area outside of the ski resort's boundaries where ski patrol does not patrol and avalanche control is not performed.

Berm = a snowbank, or a narrow path at the top or bottom of a slope, or the shoulder of a road.

Blue square = designation for intermediate trails

Bluebird day = a beautiful, clear, sunny day with a blue sky. It originally meant a day with a blue sky after a snowstorm, but now people use the phrase for any beautiful, clear day.

Black Diamond = designation for expert trail

Bumps = moguls

Bunny slope = an easier area of the ski mountain that is good for beginners because of its gentle slope.

Camber = the upward curve of the base of a ski or snowboard. The camber helps a ski to distribute the weight of a person across the ski or snowboard.

Cant = angular deviation from a plane. Slanted.

Carving = using the edge of your skis or snowboard to make a smooth turn. The edge of the ski cuts the snow like a carving knife.

Cat track = a relatively flat path across the slope

Chatter = the vibration of skis and snowboards when traveling at high speeds.

Chute = a steep and narrow passage

Cirque = similar to a bowl, but generally steeper

Corn = corn shaped snow that is the result of repeated melting and freezing.

Cornice = an overhang of snow caused by the wind

Couloir = a corridor. It is similar to a gorge or a gully, like a steep chute with walls on both sides.

Cross-country skiing = skiing done on flat terrain

Crust = a frozen layer of snow

DIN setting = the setting at which your skis will come off. In other words, how much pressure it takes for skis to come off.

Fall line = the most direct line down a slope

Freestyle = moguls with periodic jumps

Glade skiing = skiing between lots of trees

Graupel = pellets of snow. Similar to hail, except snow not ice.

Green circle = designation for beginner trails

Groomed run = manicured snow on the trail

Half pipe = a semicircular ditch made of snow. The shape is like a plumbing pipe that is cut in half (with the top half discarded) and tilted at an angle so that people can snowboard and ski down it.

Hardgoods = equipment like skis, snowboards, bindings and boots.

Hardpack = snow that has been packed down and is therefore very dense

Headwall = a steep slope at the top of a valley

Inbounds = the terrain inside the ski boundaries of a ski resort

Jib = riding a snowboard or skis across a non-snow surface like a box or a rail

Kick = how steep a jump is

Knoll = a small, rounded hill

Lip = the beginning of a steeper slope, so there is a ridge you can ski over and get a little air.

Moguls = bumps in the snow

Off-piste = out of bounds

Out of bounds = ski terrain outside of the boundaries of a ski resort

Piste = trail

Powder = fresh, dry, light snow

Promontory = a high point of land that juts out. (Technically, the high land juts out into the water, but some skiers use this term more loosely when there is no water around.)

Ski boards = ski blades = extremely short skis

Skier's left = left as you are skiing down the mountain. Opposite of Chairlift left

Skier's Right = right as you are skiing down the mountain. Opposite of Chairlift right

Skinning = walking uphill wearing skis that have skins attached to the bottom in order to make uphill travel easier. Skins inhibit sliding backwards downhill.

Softgoods = clothing

Traverse = skiing across a slope instead of skiing down

Tree line = the altitude at which trees stop growing

Tree well = a space that forms around the base of a tree after a snowfall

White out = bad visibility due to snow or fog

Wind packed = snow that wind has packed down

Zipper line = the line through the moguls that is straight down the hill, with moguls on either side.

www.ingramcontent.com/pod-product-compliance
Lightning Source LLC
Chambersburg PA
CBHW072014040426
42447CB00009B/1626

* 9 7 8 0 6 9 2 7 1 7 2 2 6 *